An Essay on the Opera / *Saggio sopra l'opera in musica*

Reproduced by courtesy of the Rijksmuseum, Amsterdam.

Pastel portrait of Francesco Algarotti by the Swiss artist Jean-Étienne Liotard

AN ESSAY ON THE OPERA /
SAGGIO SOPRA L'OPERA IN MUSICA
by Francesco Algarotti

Anonymous English Translation 1768

Edited with Notes and Introduction by
Robin Burgess

The Edwin Mellen Press
Lewiston•Queenston•Lampeter

ML
3858
A3913
2005

Library of Congress Cataloging-in-Publication Data

Algarotti, Francesco, conte, 1712-1764.
  [Saggio sopra l'opera in musica. English]
  An essay on the opera = Saggio sopra l'opera in musica / by Francesco Algarotti ; anonymous English translation 1768 ; edited with notes and introduction by Robin Burgess.
     p. cm.
  Includes bibliographical references.
  ISBN 0-7734-6048-9
  1. Opera--Philosophy and aesthetics--Early works to 1800. I. Title: Saggio sopra l'opera in musica. II. Burgess, Robin, 1949- III. Title.

ML3858.A3913 2005
782.1--dc22
                                                                              2005049597

hors série.

A CIP catalog record for this book is available from the British Library.

Front cover: The Berlin State Opera *(Deutsche Staatsoper unter den Linden)*
              © Marion Schöne, 12683 Berlin, Eichenallee 7

Copyright   ©   2005   Robin Burgess

All rights reserved. For information contact

       The Edwin Mellen Press   The Edwin Mellen Press
              Box 450   Box 67
        Lewiston, New York   Queenston, Ontario
         USA 14092-0450   CANADA L0S 1L0

              The Edwin Mellen Press, Ltd.
              Lampeter, Ceredigion, Wales
              UNITED KINGDOM SA48 8LT

            Printed in the United States of America

Contents

	Page
Acknowledgements	i
Preface by Patricia Howard	iii
Editor's Foreword	vii
Dedicatory Letter	1
Introduction	3
Chapter 1: Of the form, argument or business of an opera	9
Chapter 2: Of the musical composition for operas	17
Chapter 3: Of the recitative and singing in operas	33
Chapter 4: Of the dances	43
Chapter 5: On scenery, dress etc.	47
Chapter 6: On the structure of the theatre	57
Conclusion	65
Aeneas in Troy	69
Iphigenia in Aulis	75
A short Glossary of certain terms used in this work	103
Bibliography	107
Index of Names	111

Acknowledgements

IN preparing this edition of the contemporary English translation of Algarotti's *An Essay on the Opera*, which played a major part in the movement in mid-18th century artistic thought and endeavour that led to the evolution of a recognisably modern style of opera, best exemplified in the works of Gluck, the devotion of Patricia Howard to the latter's operas shown in several books over a period of some years has been a source of much inspiration, as my numerous citations of her work will testify. I am especially grateful to her for providing a preface and for other help generously given in conversation and letters. I must also thank Professor Julian Rushton for his assistance and for saving me from several errors.

The edition and French translation of Algarotti's essay in its 1764 version by Jean-Philippe Navarre has been an invaluable aid (see bibliography for details of this publication). M. Navarre includes the text of Marcello's *Il teatro alla moda* and relevant documents by Angiolini, the choreographer of Gluck's *Orfeo*, Metastasio and Calzabigi – Italian originals with French translations – together with an extensive letter on opera as drama by Gluck's librettist Du Roullet and musical examples by Marcello and Vinci.

Among reference works the *New Grove Dictionary of Music and Musicians*, 2nd edition, is, as always, indispensable and has been particularly helpful in tracing many of the references in Algarotti's essay.

I am grateful to the following publishers for giving permission to include extracts from copyrighted material: Oxford University Press for Patricia Howard, *Gluck: an 18th Century Portrait in Letters and Documents* and John D. Drummond, *Opera in Perspective*; Cambridge University Press for Edward J. Dent, *The Rise of Romantic Opera*, ed. Winton Dean and John Rosselli, *The Opera Industry in Italy from Cimarosa to Verdi*; Methuen Publishers for Jean Benedetti, *David Garrick and the Rise of Modern Theatre*; and Penguin Books for *Classical Literary Criticism*, ed. and tr. T. S. Dorsch. If other copyright restrictions have been inadvertently contravened, amendment will be made in any subsequent edition of this work.

The Berlin State Opera (*Deutsche Staatsoper unter den Linden*) kindly provided the cover photograph (Algarotti refers approvingly to this theatre in chapter 6 of his essay). The photo of Algarotti is from a pastel portrait by the Swiss artist Jean-Étienne Liotard reproduced by courtesy of the Rijksmuseum, Amsterdam.

Individuals whose help I should wish gratefully to acknowledge include Christelle Serre, Nina Walker, Gabriele Damiani, Edward Henley, Alan Howe, Andrea Ibba, David Jonies, Robert Quinney and Antonio Ritaccio.

R.B.

Preface

THE middle decades of the 18th century saw a lively debate over the principles and practice of opera. The origins of the debate lay in the recent invention of comic opera, which, in all its national manifestations as *opera buffa*, *opéra comique*, Ballad Opera and *Singspiel*, revealed a new approach to plot, expression and production. Critics began to measure heroic opera (which existed both as *opera seria* and *tragédie lyrique*) against the characteristics of the comic genre, and advocated the adoption of a simple narrative, uncluttered by sub-plots and minor characters, a more "natural" vocal expression, that placed more emphasis on communicating the meaning of the words rather than displaying the virtuosity of the singers, and stage movement, both for singers and dancers, that derived from the gestures of everyday life rather than from classical statuary.

There were many notable contributors to the debate. Some of these were philosophers of the arts: Antonio Planelli[1] and Esteban de Arteaga[2] in Italy, John Brown[3] and James Beattie[4] in England, and Charles de Blainville[5] and Denis Diderot[6] in France. Others were creative artists, able to put theory into practice: the librettists Ranieri de' Calzabigi[7] and François Louis du Roullet,[8] the choreographer Gasparo Angiolini,[9] the stage designer Fabrizio Galliari,[10] and a succession of bold and innovative composers, including Tommaso Traetta,[11] Christoph Gluck[12] and Mozart.[13] Algarotti's *Saggio* is central to the debate: it

---

[1] *Dell' opere in musica*, 1772.
[2] *Le rivoluzioni del teatro musicale italiano dalla sua origine fine al presente*, 1783.
[3] *A Dissertation on the Rise, Union and Power, the Progressions, Separations and Corruptions of Poetry and Music*, 1763.
[4] *Essay on Poetry and Music as They Affect the Mind*, 1778.
[5] *L'esprit de l'art musical*, 1754.
[6] *De la poésie dramatique*, 1773.
[7] *Alceste*, 1767.
[8] *Iphigénie en Aulide*, 1774.
[9] *Don Juan*, 1761.
[10] *Alceste*, 1767.
[11] *Ifigenia in Tauride*, 1763.
[12] *Alceste*, 1767.
[13] *Idomeneo*, 1781.

deals with all the major issues; it was the most widely quoted of all the texts; and it addresses opera both as a philosophical conundrum and as a living theatrical experience. Although he was concerned with the theory of each constituent part of opera, Algarotti's writing reveals much practical experience in the opera house. He is knowledgeable about voices and orchestras. His advice on theatre construction from the point of view of design, acoustics and sight-lines is still valid. And he supported his criticism of contemporary librettos by offering two models (neither of which was ever set): a detailed scenario for *Enea in Troia* and a complete libretto (in French) for *Iphigénie en Aulide*.

At the heart of the debate on opera was the often expressed desire to return opera to its inspirational origins – the simplicity and power of ancient Greek drama. Algarotti in particular was seized by this neo-classical agenda. It must, of course, be pure coincidence that the first edition of the *Saggio* was published in the same year that the pioneer of neo-classicism, the art historian Johann Joachim Winckelmann, undertook his momentous journey to Rome. Algarotti's essay is, however, infused by the same passionate rediscovery of the noble simplicity, balance and order of classical art. Like Winckelmann, Algarotti might well have said that it was only after contemplating examples of classical beauty that he learned what it was to be alive.

Although the various editions of Algarotti's essay in the original Italian have recently been published in facsimile,[14] the English translation of the 1763 edition has never been reprinted, and copies are rare outside the big research libraries. It deserves to be better known. It is essential reading for anyone investigating currents in Enlightenment philosophy that relate to opera, and moreover the translation, tantalisingly anonymous, is an especially engaging one, evoking at times the vigorous expression of a Fielding or a Smollett, at others the appealing directness of a Goldsmith (whom the editor cautiously proposes as the identity of the translator). I particularly welcome this carefully edited edition. Algarotti peopled his text with many references to 18th century personalities, some celebrated, some obscure: it is good to have these explained in the editorial footnotes, together with the additional resource of Algarotti's footnotes from the edition of 1764. Heroic opera is still a misunderstood genre. Commentaries such as Algarotti's can only deepen our knowledge of its reception in its own time and our understanding of how one acutely sensitive contemporary enthusiast could find in it that 'combination of a thousand pleasures ... so extraordinary <that> our world has nothing to equal it.'[15]

Dr. Patricia Howard
(formerly Lecturer and Tutor in Music
at the Open University, Milton Keynes, U.K.)

---

[14] See bibliography.
[15] Below, p. 66.

Editor's Foreword

And what is worse than all, now that the Manager has monopolized the Opera House, haven't we the Signors and Signioras calling here, sliding their smooth semibreves, and gargling glib divisions in their outlandish throats – with foreign emissaries and French spies, for aught I know, disguised like fiddles and figure dancers!

MRS. DANGLE complaining to her husband in Sheridan's witty parody of theatrical conventions, *The Critic*, of 1779 expresses a typically robust and commonsensical English aversion to that 'exotic and irrational entertainment' of opera (in Dr. Johnson's famous dictum), which never perhaps was more exotic and irrational than in the first half of the 18th century. A later scene in the play reflects Sheridan's own experience of managing an opera house - the King's Theatre in the Haymarket, scene of Handel's successes - and dealing with temperamental singers. Nevertheless it was those 'Signors and Signioras' with their smooth semibreves and glib divisions, and their temperament, who made Italian opera the height of fashion throughout the length and breadth of Europe (with the notable exception of France) - from London to Lisbon, Stockholm to St. Petersburg - so much so that no noble court or proudly independent free city was complete without its resident troupe of Italian singers.

Opera seria, as it was called, retold stories from classical mythology or ancient history in a strictly regulated sequence - three arias for the *prima donna* for every two for the *seconda donna* and so on - features which have made this form of opera seem in recent times to be excessively stilted and formal, its characters little more than cardboard cut-outs, the amorous intrigues in which they become embroiled absurd fantastications.[16]

---

[16] John D. Drummond makes the significant point that contemporary criticisms of *opera seria* are determined by '20th century theatrical experiences, born of 19th century melodrama and fostered by the commercial cinema' (*Opera in Perspective*, London 1980, p.359, footnote 4 to ch. 5). If approached on its own terms and with understanding of its conventions, *opera seria* 'can speak to our own condition in a very powerful way, even more powerful perhaps than the spectacle of John Wayne rescuing a stage-coach from marauding Indians'! Drummond's chapter on *opera seria* offers an insightful discussion of the form, showing that it can provide as valid an experience of

And yet this was "serious" opera, Zeno's and Metastasio's reform of the degenerate state into which opera had lapsed after the early 17th century experiments to revive in modern Europe the spirit *and* the letter of Classical Greek drama, in which, as was known, music played a prominent part. In our day to be sure the operas of Handel, the greatest practitioner of *opera seria,* have been revived with considerable success (though often in productions which seem to undermine, rather than illuminate, the form – an implicit admission of lack of confidence in it), but more, one suspects, for their musical riches than their dramatic appeal.

Herein lies the dilemma: instead of achieving a convincing and coherent union of music and drama in one integrated art-form (the project of the Florentine and Paduan academicians who created opera in the 1600s), *opera seria* segregated the delineation of the plot to the musically simple *secco* (dry) recitative, while the composer and singer were allowed full play in the arias where the progress of the drama had for all intents and purposes come to a full stop. When the outstanding abilities of its star singers were still fresh this essential incongruity probably counted for little, but as time went on it became more and more apparent for those who cared about opera as music-drama - and let us not forget that *opera seria* enjoyed fashionable acclaim for half a century and continued to be written as late as Mozart's final opera, *La clemenza di Tito,* in 1791 (although, one might add, Metastasio's libretto was much altered – 'turned into a real opera,' as Mozart put it – by his librettist Mazzolà).

Criticism appeared in, for example, Benedetto Marcello's amusing pamphlet *Il teatro alla moda* of 1720, which satirised contemporary operatic practice, and in productions like *The Beggar's Opera* at London in 1728, deliberately set among the low life of highwaymen and pickpockets to contrast with the nobly magnanimous personages of *opera seria.* There was also to come implicit internal criticism in the shape of interesting experiments in new forms of aria or recitative,

---

musical drama as Gluckian reform opera. It will be apparent in reading his essay that Algarotti's criticisms are directed at features of performing practice as much as at the form itself.

or in enterprising orchestration, in the work of composers like Niccolò Jommelli and Tommaso Traetta. These two Neapolitan-trained musicians anticipated the reform opera of Gluck, Traetta serving for several years at the court of Parma where Algarotti was at one time involved in the direction of theatrical spectacles. The latter's *Essay on the Opera* was described by Ernest Newman[17] as 'the most remarkable book on the opera' of its day. Its author was equally one of the age's most remarkable men.

Francesco Algarotti was born at Venice on 11 December 1712 of a family of wealthy merchants. He was to become one of his native city's most characteristic children, a versatile and accomplished connoisseur of the arts and sciences who, according to Alfonso Lowe, was called 'everything from busybody to *uomo universale.*'[18] Apart from the Classics his education at Rome and Bologna included studies in science, philosophy and mathematics and was completed, in typical 18th century fashion, by a Grand Tour of Europe. In 1735 he visited Paris, becoming acquainted, among others, with Voltaire and the mathematician Pierre Maupertuis. The latter asked Algarotti to join an expedition he was organising to Lapland to test an implication of the newly fashionable Newtonian physics, the flattening of the earth at its poles. Algarotti was already a convinced supporter of Newton, having championed him in Bologna against the anti-Newtonian views of one Rizzetti, and was engaged in writing his own popular exposition of Newton's physics. Instead of going to Lapland with Maupertuis, however, he preferred - understandably perhaps - to accept an invitation to visit Voltaire and his mistress, Émilie du Châtelet, at her estate of Cirey. Émilie, who made an admired French translation of the Latin of Newton's *Principia Mathematica,* and was an early advocate of female scholarship, expressly learned Italian to be able to be converse with her guest, while Algarotti for his part somewhat unkindly repaid her hospitality by portraying her in his book as a flighty Marchioness who is initiated into the mysteries of Newton's physics in a series of dialogues with her male

---

[17] In *Gluck and the Opera: a Study in Musical History,* London 1895, p.232.
[18] See *La Serenissima: the Last Flowering of the Venetian Repulic*, London 1974, p.56.

tutor.[19] The work was published in 1737 as *Eccovi il Newtonianismo per le Dame*, its dialogue form being one Algarotti was to use again in treating of a variety of other learned matters: an English translation by Elizabeth Carter, one of the original Bluestockings, appeared two years later.

From Paris Algarotti went on to London, where he came to know such luminaries of the day as Pope, Hume and Garrick. Another (unhappy) friendship was with Lady Mary Wortley Montagu, by no means the only person to be captivated by Algarotti's urbanity and physical handsomeness (Volaire's possibly ironic sobriquet for him was my *cher cygne de Padoue* - 'dear swan of Padua') and to suffer for his sake the pains of unrequited love. Alongside romantic imbroglios, however, Algarotti clearly read widely in English letters - to judge at least from the number of references in his essay on opera, some of them to writers now little known.

In the company of Lord Baltimore Algarotti continued his European tour to Holland, Denmark and Sweden, relating their further experiences and impressions in a series of letters to Lord John Hervey published as *Travels in Russia*. It was on returning from St. Petersburg to Prussia that there occurred in 1740 one of the most momentous meetings in Algarotti's career - with the Crown Prince Frederick at his house in Rheinsberg. Nancy Mitford describes the effect Algarotti had on the future king in these terms: 'of the same age as Frederick, he had that Italian polish - a combination of the manners, tact and intelligence of an ancient race, a childlike *joie de vivre* and an easy sexuality - that operates so powerfully on the less sophisticated Northerner.'[20] Although this initial attraction seems to have worn thin rather quickly and their friendship was to suffer various vicissitudes, Frederick remained devoted to Algarotti for over twenty years, awarding him the title of count and a new order *pour le mérite* and engaging him on a diplomatic mission to the court of Turin.

---

[19] See Patricia Fara, *Newton: the Making of Genius*, London 2003, pp.135f. This study explores *inter alia* the contemporary reception of Newton's theories by the European scientific community, especially in France.
[20] *Frederick the Great*, London 1970, p.76.

During his time in Berlin Algarotti advised on opera productions and adapted Italian librettos, while also writing poetry and essays on a variety of subjects. The operas in question included works by Frederick's favoured composer, Carl Heinrich Graun, one of the leading German practitioners of *opera seria*, who, partly at the king's prompting, was to introduce some modest departures from prevailing conventions, e.g. a less marked dependence on the characteristic *da capo* aria-form in his *Semiramide* of 1754 and *Montezuma* of the following year (the later work is mentioned approvingly by Algarotti in chapter 1 of his essay).

After a falling-out with Frederick[21] Algarotti spent the years 1742 to 1747 as artistic adviser to the Elector Augustus III of Saxony, who had continued his father, Augustus the Strong's ideal of developing their capital city of Dresden into one of the jewels of civilised Europe. The 'Florence on the Elbe,' ironically, was to be destroyed as effectively by Prussian bombardment in the Seven Years' War as it was by Allied bombing in 1945. Frederick wrote to Algarotti in 1760, 'Miserable madmen that we are: with only a moment to live we make that moment as harsh as we can; amusing ourselves with the destruction of the masterpieces of industry and of time, we leave an odious memory of our ravages and the calamities which they cause.'[22]

It was thanks to Algarotti's patronage that Italian painters such as his fellow-Venetians Pittoni, Piazzetta, Amigoni and especially Tiepolo (whose European fame owes much to Algarotti's advocacy) were commissioned to add to the collections of the famous *Gemäldegalerie* in Dresden, the first such work being Tiepolo's *Banquet of Cleopatra*.[23] Alfonso Lowe comments that with his

---

[21] According to Nancy Mitford (*op. cit.*, p.125), Frederick 'wrote to Algarotti saying that his apparition at Berlin would be like that of the *aurora borealis*, but, never being able to resist teasing the Italian, he added, "You would be especially welcome if you came for my sake and not for that of Plutus." It was too much for Algarotti, who cheekily replied that far from being attracted by Plutus he had found his last visit to the King in Silesia very expensive indeed. Frederick was furious and though Algarotti wrote a grovelling apology five years elapsed before they made it up.'
[22] Nancy Mitford, *op. cit.*, p.200. She adds, 'the difference is that in the 18th century a town could be rebuilt as beautiful as ever; now it cannot.' Thirty years on, with the 21st century reconstruction of Dresden, that observation is happily being controverted.
[23] Royal Academy of Arts, *Masterpieces from Dresden*, exhibition catalogue, London 2003, p.109.

insistence on historical correctness in the painting of Classical scenes Algarotti was able to make suggestions that led to the improvement of this and other works.[24] He made a present of another work of Tiepolo's, *Maecenas presenting the Liberal Arts to Caesar Augustus* (now in the Hermitage Museum, St. Petersburg), to the Elector's prime minister, Count Heinrich von Brühl, a fellow-connoisseur and collector of paintings, keeping a watercolour copy in his own home. Maecenas is shown introducing to the emperor three female figures, accompanied by the poet Homer, who symbolise the arts of painting, sculpture and architecture: in the background can be seen Brühl's own palace and gardens in Dresden. One can sense the iconic significance of this scene for Algarotti himself seeing that he, as much as Brühl, out of his devotion to 'the masterpieces of industry and of time' played the role of patron of the arts at the Prussian and Saxon courts: he and Frederick even called each other *Mécène* and *Auguste*.

For reasons of ill-health and aversion to the Northern climate Algarotti returned in 1753 to Italy, living first in Venice and Bologna and settling finally in Pisa. As we have seen he had assisted with the staging of theatrical works at Berlin and Dresden. On returning to his homeland he was invited by Guillaume du Tillot, minister at the Bourbon court of Parma, to collaborate with the composer Traetta and his librettist Frugoni in a reform of opera that would bring together elements of both French and Italian practice. The first product of this movement, by common consent only a moderate success, was the *Ippolito ed Aricia* of 1759 by Traetta, its libretto modelled on that of Jean-Philippe Rameau's first Paris opera of 1733 (it also uses some of Rameau's music). It was followed in 1760 by Traetta's *I Tindaridi* with libretto adapted from that of Rameau's second major opera, *Castor et Pollux,* of 1737. The French *tragédie lyrique,* first devised by Lully for the court of Louis XIV and raised to new heights of powerful and even tragic dramatic expression by Rameau, especially in the two works mentioned and the later *Dardanus*, was the only form of serious opera in Europe to rival the dominance of *opera seria*, and although confined in performance to France itself

---

[24] Alfonso Lowe, *op. cit.,* p.56.

its influence on the Italian school through works like Traetta's was not inconsiderable. Its fusion of music, dancing and stage spectacle provided an important model for the reform operas of Gluck, the last and finest of whose works were written in French and designed for Paris,[25] and can even be said to prefigure the Wagnerian *Gesamtkunstwerk*.

During his final years in Italy, as well as carrying on an extensive correspondence with major personalities of the time, Algarotti worked on a wide variety of essays on different subjects - questions of language, literature, the fine arts of painting and architecture, history, philosophy and economics. His writings were collected in nine volumes between 1764 and 1765, some of them, like the essay on opera having been continuously refined over some years and going through several editions. The essay form would seem to be well suited to a writer of Algarotti's type: not perhaps particularly original in his judgments, but one who had an intimate and thorough knowledge of many of the important currents of contemporary thought and its leading exponents and who could deploy new ideas with the support of his own variegated experience and precise and acute personal observations. Certain features of his character and temperament may suggest a touch of dilettantism; the essays show the hand of a true scholar - one who could still, before the age of specialisation, encompass the entire range of artistic and scientific endeavour.

Algarotti died on 3 May 1764 at the age of 52. Frederick had a tombstone made for him with this epitaph:

---

[25] Gluck's début in Paris in 1774 was with his *Iphigénie en Aulide*, regarded by Algarotti, as it was by Diderot, as an exemplary subject for an opera. Algarotti's own French libretto for such an opera is included as an appendix to his essay. It may be compared with Du Roullet's libretto for Gluck, likewise based on Racine's *Iphigénie*. (Alfonso Lowe (*loc. cit.*) mentions a less successful example of Algarotti's librettistic efforts, the operetta *Il congresso di Citera*, which depicts 'a council of nations meeting to discuss the right way to make love,' arguing for the superiority of hedonism: according to Lowe it stands out for its 'sheer stupidity').

ALGAROTTO OVIDII AEMULO, NEUTONI DISCIPULO FREDERICUS REX.[26]

The work of Algarotti's that remains his best known in the republic of letters as a whole is the dialogue on Newtonian physics intended for the enlightenment of gentlewomen. The one that may, through its clear prefigurement of the Gluckian reform opera, have had the greatest practical influence,[27] is the essay on opera, which is clearly the outcome of both sustained reflection on the opera form and of Algarotti's own experience in the theatre. Its first edition was published at Venice in 1755 and a later revised and expanded edition at Leghorn in 1763.[28] There was to be a further revised version in the collected edition of 1764.[29]

The essay sets out a detailed programme examining each of opera's constituent elements in turn from the point of view above all of dramatic expression and cogency: Algarotti even considers the design of the opera-house and the most suitable materials for its construction (wood being his choice for the interior, cp. the *Festspielhaus* at Bayreuth). His starting-point is the realisation that only a differently arranged type of libretto can overcome the dramatic weakness of *opera seria*. It was indeed the new style of libretto of Ranieri de' Calzabigi, with its condensed mythological plot dispensing with the minor characters and confusing sub-plots of *opera seria*, and its use of chorus and ballet as integrated, rather than decorative, elements in the dramatic development, that made possible the success

---

[26] 'Frederick the King <dedicated this stone> to Algarotti, rival of Ovid and disciple of Newton': quoted in Lowe, *op. cit.,* p.56. The grave is in the Campo Santo of Pisa.
[27] Patricia Howard, *Christoph Willibald Gluck: a Guide to Research*, 2nd edition, London 2003, lists two studies that particularly focus on the influence of Algarotti's ideas: Karl Geiringer, *Concepts of the Enlightenment as reflected in Gluck's Italian Reform Operas* in *Studies in Voltaire and the 18th Century* 88 (1972), pp.567-576 (item 176) and Egon Wellesz, *Francesco Algarotti und seine Stellung zu Musik* in *Sommelbände der Internationalen Musikgesellschaft* 15 (1913-14), pp.427-439 (item 273).
[28] For the textual history see Francesco Algarotti: *Saggio sopra l'opera in musica: Le edizioni del 1755 e del 1763,* ed. Annalisa Bini in the series *Libreria Italiana Musicale Editrice,* Rome 1989, pp.xi-xxii. This volume contains facsimile reprints of the two editions with an informative introduction by Signorina Bini.
[29] The publisher of the latter two editions was Marco Coltellini, himself a librettist of reform operas including Gluck's *Telemaco* and Traetta's *Ifigenia in Tauride* and *Antigona*. He also revised Goldoni's libretto of *La finta semplice* for music by the twelve-year-old Mozart.

of Gluck's *Orfeo ed Euridice* (Vienna 1762) and Gluck himself was to acknowledge his indebtedness to his librettist.[30] It is probable that Gluck or at least Calzabigi knew Algarotti's essay, since phrases from the celebrated preface to *Alceste*[31] seem to derive from it (some of these resemblances will be pointed out in the notes to Algarotti's text). The so-called reform opera which began with *Orfeo*, continued with *Alceste* and *Paride ed Elena* - all three Italian operas for Vienna with libretti by Calzabigi - and reached its finest flowering in the Paris operas of the 1770s, among them the revised *Orphée* and *Alceste,* the seemingly archaic but otherwise revolutionary *Armide*, and culminating in Gluck's crowning masterpiece *Iphigénie en Tauride,* is certainly the clearest and most successful implementation of Algarotti's intentions for a true music-drama. His essay can, however, stand in its own right as an outstanding contribution to operatic theory and above all to the idea that truth to nature and naturalness are indispensable elements in any art-form that seeks to be humanly affecting.

As an example of Algarotti's elegant Italian style I include the dedicatory epistle to William Pitt the Elder which appeared in the 1763 version, replacing the original dedication to Baron von Sweerts, director of theatrical spectacles at the court of Berlin:

Sembrerà ad alcuni assai strano, che a Vos, *Uomo immortale, che nella vostra nazione sapeste riaccendere il nativo valore, sapeste proveder per sempre alla sua difesa, e la faceste in un medesimo anno trionfare nelle quattro parti del Mondo, venga intitulato uno scritto, che ragiona di Poesia, di Musica, di cose di Teatro. Ma pare che ignorino costoro, come il Restitutore dell' Inghilterra, l'amico del gran FEDERICO sa ancora munire il suo ozio co' presidi delle Lettere, e come quella sua vittoriosa eloquenza, colla quale egli tuona in Senato, non è meno l'effetto della elevatezza del suo animo, che dello studio da lui posto*

---

[30] E.g. in his letter to the *Mercure de France,* 1 February 1773: 'I would be ... seriously to blame if I were to take the credit for the invention of a new genre of Italian opera, the attempt at which has been vindicated by success: the principal merit belongs to M. de Calzabigi. And if my music has had some acclaim, I must acknowledge my debt to him, because it is he who set me on the path to develop the resources of my art' (tr. in Patricia Howard, *Gluck: an 18th Century Portrait in Letters and Documents,* Oxford 1995, p.106).

[31] A letter dedicating the score published at Vienna in 1769 to the Archduke Leopold of Tuscany and setting out what is in effect a manifesto of the new style. Although signed by Gluck, it is usually thought to have been written by Calzabigi: for text see Howard, *op. cit.,* pp.84f.

nei Tulli, e nei Demosteni antecessori suoi. Possa solamente questo mio Scritto esser da tanto, che trovi anch' esso un luogo nell' ozio erudito di un tal Uomo, e giunga ad ottenere il suffragio di Colui, che ne' più alti uffizi della Stato ha meritato ammirazione e l'applauso di tutta Europa.[32]

The English translation by an anonymous writer of the 1763 version of Algarotti's essay which follows was published at Glasgow in 1768, a virtual reprint of a London publication of the previous year. The copy from which I worked is in the Bodleian Library, Oxford. I have to some extent modernised the orthography and punctuation and included footnotes and other additions that Algarotti made to the later 1764 edition of his essay when these seemed of particular interest: for the most part they are illustrative quotations, sometimes lengthy, from other writers. All footnotes are indicated by consecutive superior numbers. Where the footnote is Algarotti's own it is introduced as [Author's note:] or [Author's note 1764:] with my own additions in square [ ] brackets. There are a few minor divergences and omissions from the original Italian text which I have noted where they might be of significance.

For the sake of completeness I have included the glossary at the end of the English version. Annalisa Bini[33] remarks on the peculiarity of this glossary which seems to have been added by the English editor or translator for the benefit of a reading public unfamiliar with musical terminology: would such an audience be attracted to an essay like this? (Considering the obscurity of some of the definitions, one might also question its usefulness). She does, however, also acknowledge the faithfulness of the translation.

Algarotti's essay was in fact disseminated widely in the cultivated circles of his day. The English translation was the first, but it was followed by translations into German, French (a somewhat embroidered version by François Jean de Chastellux, himself a theorist of opera and theatre) and Spanish - a tribute to its

---

[32] For translation *v. infra*, p.1.
[33] *Op. cit.*, p.xli.

contemporary interest and respect for its author; a sign also, by contrast, of his corresponding and undeserved neglect today.

The following table summarises the publication history of the essay and its translations in the 18th century:[34]

1755	*Discorso sopra l'opera in musica* in *Discorsi sopra differenti soggetti*, published by Giambattista Pasquali[35]	Venice
1755	*Saggio sopra l'opera in musica*: the above retitled and published separately, probably by Pasquali	[Venice]
1757	*Saggio sopra l'opera in musica*: the above included in the second of two volumes of *Opere varie* of Algarotti, published by Pasquali	Venice
1763	*Saggio sopra l'opera in musica*: revised version, published by Marco Coltellini	Leghorn
1764	*Saggio sopra l'opera in musica*: the previous entry further revised and included in the second of nine volumes of the collected *Opere* of Algarotti, published by Coltellini	Leghorn
1767	*An Essay on the Opera*: English translation of the *Saggio*, published by L. Davis and C. Reymers	London
1768	*An Essay on the Opera*: the previous entry republished by R. Urie	Glasgow
1769	*Saggio sopra l'opera in musica* in German translation by Johann Friedrich Hemmerde, published by Rudolf Erich Raspe	Kassel
1773	*Saggio sopra l'opera in musica* in French translation by François Jean de Chastellux	Paris
1787	*Saggio sopra l'opera in musica* in Spanish translation by Manuel Escribano	Madrid

Note on the authorship of the translation

There seems to be no evidence for the identity of the anonymous translator, so one can only speculate who he or she may have been. An obvious candidate must be Elizabeth Carter, who translated Algarotti's earlier work on Newton's optics and was adept in Italian and several other languages. She was criticised for the over-elegant style of her work on the Stoic philosopher Epictetus, for whom

---

[34] Information from Annalisa Bini, *op. cit.*, pp. xi-xii and xl-xlvi.
[35] The title page carries the motto *Dulces ante omnia Musae* (the Muses are sweet above all things) and a decorative vignette of a lyre and compasses. For the reprint in the same year the epigraph is changed to the quotation from Ovid cited in footnote 101. This is retained in 1763, when the vignette is varied with the addition of an owl.

something rougher was considered more appropriate, and certainly a marked characteristic of the translation of the essay on opera is the beautiful quality of its 18th century English prose. Mrs. Carter produced no more books for publication after 1766, before the first edition of the translation, and is not known for any particular interest in music or the theatre, but she was clearly capable of this work.

Another possibility, that can admittedly only be regarded as a most tentative conjecture, is that the author was Oliver Goldsmith. He was well versed in the French language and in French literature, and is credited with translations from French and Latin. There seem to be no known translations he made from Italian, but he did in his earlier years spend five months on a walking tour of northern Italy, living from hand to mouth, so that he would in all likelihood have picked up at least a working knowledge of the language. As an accomplished Classicist he might not have had overmuch difficulty in coping with Algarotti's literary Italian, perhaps seeking specialist scholarly help where needed.

Goldsmith's first published work to achieve any recognition was his *Enquiry into the Present State of Polite Learning in Europe* of 1759, a conspectus of the current state of the arts and literature. The chapter on Italy suggests that after Metastasio and Maffei writers deserving the highest applause include Zeno, Algarotti, Goldoni and Muratori. The latter is mentioned by Algarotti himself in the essay on opera as one of the leaders of civilised taste.

Later in the same year Goldsmith wrote eight numbers of an occasional journal called *The Bee*, in which there appeared a piece on the opera in England. In it he criticises singers for the extravagant coloratura excesses characteristic of the performance of *opera seria* such as are also deprecated by Algarotti and the preface to *Alceste*. Goldsmith suggests that composers should cultivate a greater simplicity, as for example Rameau sometimes does. Professor A. Lytton Sells[36] claims that Goldsmith had no particular interest in music or opera, but could give the appearance of knowing a great deal about them. We can at any rate state that

---

[36] In *Oliver Goldsmith: his Life and Works,* London 1974. For Goldsmith's views on opera see pp.89f.; for the *Enquiry* pp.208f.

he was acquainted with Algarotti's work and expressed similar misgivings about the state of opera in his day.

By 1767, when the English translation of the essay on opera was published at London, Goldsmith was already known as the author of the poem *The Traveller* and the novel *The Vicar of Wakefield* (a favourite book, as it happens, of Gluck, who was an avid reader of English novels in translation). The following year saw the first performance of Goldsmith's comedy *The Good-natured Man*. One might, therefore, expect his name to be attached to any other work appearing at this time, but it was then not uncommon for translations, essays, magazine articles and the like to be issued anonymously, even when they were by established authors. Goldsmith might well have regarded the book as journeyman work undertaken only for financial gain (he was habitually short of cash), though that did not prevent him lavishing on such projects all his considerable literary art.

Like Mrs. Carter - perhaps even more so - Goldsmith is of course a master of Classical English prose style and more than capable of the attractive period quality of the translation. In default of any certainty those who wish may consider it reasonable to imagine that he could have been its author.

To WILLIAM PITT

FRANCESCO ALGAROTTI

THAT to you, immortal man, who knew how to rekindle in your nation her native valour, to provide for her perpetual defence, and caused her to triumph in one year in the four quarters of the globe,[37] a treatise on poetry, music and theatrical subjects should be addressed will to some appear strange.

But these, it would seem, are not apprised that the restorer of England, the friend of the great Frederick,[38] knows also to invigorate his leisure with the powers of literature, and that that victorious eloquence with which he thunders in the senate proceeds no less from the elevation of his mind than from his studies in Tully[39] and Demosthenes, his predecessors. May this treatise even find place in the leisure of such a man and obtain the suffrage of one who, in the highest offices of the state, has deserved the admiration and applause of all Europe!

Pisa, 18 December 1762.

---

[37] Pitt the Elder's accession to power in 1757 after early British reverses in the Seven Years' War was the occasion of his famous remark, 'I am sure I can save this nation, and nobody else can.' It is indeed to his leadership and policy that British success in the conflict has been largely attributed. Considering that the war involved all the major European powers and extended to North America, the Caribbean, Africa and India 'the four quarters of the globe' is little exaggeration.

[38] Britain had entered into agreement with Prussia by the treaty of Westminster in 1756 to guarantee the neutrality of Hanover, thus increasing the likelihood of hostility from France and Austria and of the outbreak of war. In changing the original dedication of his essay, therefore, Algarotti was recognising a political ally of his own patron, Frederick the Great, at the height of his (Pitt's) career.

[39] I.e. Cicero, one of the foremost Roman orators, as Demosthenes was among the Greeks.

INTRODUCTION

NO method more effectual hath been imagined by human invention to afford a delightful entertainment to ingenuous minds than that all-accomplished and harmonious performance by way of excellence called *opera*; because in forming it no article was forgotten, no means omitted, no ingredient left unemployed that could in any shape contribute to so important an end: and indeed it may with reason be affirmed that the most powerful charms of music, of the mimic art, of dancing and of painting are in operatical performances all happily combined, that they may conspire in a friendly manner to refine our sentiments, to soothe the heart and subdue the stubbornness of reason that cannot help surrendering itself a willing captive to so pleasing a fascination.

But from the very concurrence of so many requisites it happens in like manner to the opera, as it does to the most complicated machines, to be thence liable to frequent failures and being out of order. Nor indeed should it be a cause of surprise to us if so ingenious a composition, and resulting from the combination of so many parts as an opera does, should not always answer the end proposed, although no care, pains or study to attain perfection had been omitted by those to whom the preparation of such an entertainment was intrusted.

It must however be confessed that the persons who nowadays take upon them the guidance of those public diversions do neither enter into a due consideration of particulars, nor pay a proper attention to the several necessary constituents for making an opera perfect; nay, upon examination they will be found remiss in choosing the subject of their dramas and still more negligent about the words thereof being congenially adapted for the music that is to accompany them. These gentlemen appear to be entirely careless of verisimilitude in the singing and recitative parts, as well as about the connection that ought to subsist between the intervening ballets executed by the dancers and the main business of the drama. The former should seem to spring genuinely from the latter. They are equally regardless of appropriate decorations in the scenery department; and the faulty structure of their theatres hitherto hath quite escaped their notice. What wonder then if that species of dramatic representation which, from its nature, ought to prove the most delightful of all scenic entertainments hath degenerated to such a degree of insipidity and irksomeness to spectators in general![40]

Through a defect of that harmony which should always prevail among the several parts of which an opera is composed there now hardly remains even a faint shadow of that true imitation and agreeable illusion which can only result from a perfect consonance among them. By such neglects hath the opera (originally one of the most ingenious combinations the human mind could pride itself for) dwindled into a languid, badly connected, improbable, grotesque and monstrous aggregate;[41] wherefore it has too justly incurred the evil fame that was spread against it and the stigmatising censures of many respectable personages who otherwise very judiciously considered innocent amusements, when tastefully directed, as matters of no small moment or indifference to a well regulated government.[42]

---

[40] Cf. the preface to *Alceste*: the abuses to which Italian opera has been subject have 'turned the most sumptuous and beautiful of all spectacles into the most ridiculous and the most tedious' (in Patricia Howard, *Gluck: an 18th Century Portrait in Letters and Documents,* Oxford 1995, p.84).

[41] As opera, intended by its creators to be a revival of classical Greek drama, became in Italy a popular entertainment, so its original purpose was forgotten and operas came to be little more than a pretext for a spectacular stage pageant. Martin Cooper (*Gluck,* London 1935, pp.7f.) records the constituents of Freschi's *Berenice* of 1680: choruses of virgins, soldiers and horsemen; various instrumentalists including six mounted trumpeters; several chariots drawn by live horses etc. etc. As he says, it is 'more suggestive of a circus' than a musical drama.

[42] [Author's note:] Among the many unfavourable opinions against operas which may be cited is the following from an eminent English writer, and runs thus. – 'As the waters of a certain fountain of Thessaly, from their benumbing quality, could be contained in nothing but the hoof of an ass, so can this languid and disjointed composition (the opera) find no admittance but in such heads as are expressly formed to receive it' (*The World,* No. 156 [under the pseudonym of 'Philonus']). - A long time prior to this censure had the judicious Addison applied for motto to the fifth number of the first volume of *The Spectator* (where he treats of the Italian opera) this verse from Horace:

Spectatum admissi risum teneatis amici?

['(If a painter wished to join a horse's neck to a human head ...), would you, friends, if admitted to a viewing, hold back your laughter?' – *de Arte Poetica,* v.5.

It is the incongruity of 'joining together inconsistencies and making the decoration partly real and partly imaginary' that Addison particularly criticises in the essay cited. In a later number of *The Spectator*, Vol. 1 No. 18, he deprecates the mixing of languages, English and Italian, in the singing of operas and claims that 'if the Italians have a genius for music above the English, the English have a genius for other performances of a much higher nature and capable of giving the

But to restore the opera to its pristine dignity and estimation is, in my sense, an undertaking now as necessary to be attempted as it may prove difficult to be carried into execution. The attempt I propose here is to reduce the musical province into a proper regulation and to make the performers learn a due obedience to discipline and authority.[43] For how is it to be expected that a drama, although written in ever so masterly a manner, can be exhibited with the requisite propriety if the judgment of those who ought to preside should be disregarded? Nay more, how can we harbour even the least hope of enjoying the laudable composition of a drama if those persons who by their situation should listen to and obey the direction of their superiors in sense, notwithstanding their disqualification, arrogate to themselves the power of dictating and issuing their mandates? In fine, how can we propose to ourselves that any good effect should

---

mind a much nobler entertainment,' and in vol. 1 no. 29 he discusses the inappropriateness of the Italian recitative style to the setting of English words. In this number also he praises the work of Lully and closes with the observation that music and the other arts 'are to deduce their laws and rules from the general sense and taste of mankind and not from the principles of those arts themselves, or in other words the taste is not to conform to the art, but the art to the taste. Music is not designed to please only chromatic ears, but all that are capable of distinguishing harsh from disagreeable notes. A man of an ordinary ear is a judge whether a passion is expressed in proper sounds and whether the melody of those sounds be more or less pleasing' – an example of Johnsonian commonsense as applied to opera.]

And before him Dryden had said in some verses to Sir Godfrey Kneller,

> For what a song or senseless opera
> Is to the living labour of a play,
> Or what a play to Virgil's work would be,
> Such is a single piece to history.

[vv.150-153. Dryden regrets that he himself, like Kneller, is compelled by the times to labour on slight subjects, so that their works like contemporary opera must appear insignificant in comparison with Virgil or the Italian painters whose art Kneller saw on his youthful travels to Italy. The poem appeared in *The Ancient Miscellany* of 1694: for complete text see *The Poems of John Dryden*, ed. John Kinsley, Oxford 1958, Vol. II, pp.858-863.

In the 1764 edition Algarotti added this further quotation:] And St. Évremond in Vol. III of his works: *Une sottise chargée de Musique, de Danse, de Machines, des Décorations, est une sottise magnifique, mais toujours sottise.* [A species of foolishness filled with music, dancing, devices and decorations may be magnificent, but it is still foolishness.]

[43] [Author's note 1764:] καὶ γὰρ ὅταν ἡμῖν βουλώμεθα ἀγωνίζεσθαι, ἆθλα μὲν ὁ ἄρχων προτίθησιν, ἀθροίζειν δὲ αὐτοὺς προσέτακται χορηγοῖς, καὶ ἄλλους διδάσκειν, καὶ ἀνάγκην προστιθέναι τοῖς ἐνδεῶς τι ποιοῦσιν. Xenophon, *Hiero* 9.1. [When we want to have a choral competition, the archon sets the prizes, but chorus-masters are given the task of bringing the choirs together, while others are deputed to train the choirs and exercise discipline over those who fall short in any respect.]

result from the disorderliness of a mutinous band of people, so obstinately averse from filling those stations in an opera to which their nature had best adapted them? What frequent acts of flight and misbehaviour are observable towards the poet, who from the right reason of things ought to superintend the whole and act as chief pilot to steer their vessel to the harbour of success.

What frequent jealousies and wranglings arise among the singers on account of one person's having more ariettas than another, a loftier plume,[44] a longer and more flowing robe etc., all which frivolous disputes are often more perplexing to be settled than the ceremonial to be observed at a congress or the precedency of ambassadors from different courts.[45]

The first step then necessary to be taken in order to remove such abuses is that the poet should resume the reins of power which have been so unjustly wrested from his hands; and that, being restored to his rightful authority, he may diffuse through every department good order and due subordination.

What legislator would take upon him to give new laws to a people, whirled about in the confusion of anarchy, until such time as their natural magistrates were replaced on their tribunals and homage paid to their power? What general would march to attack an enemy if he had not previously banished disorder and licentiousness from his army?

---

[44] The castrato Marchesi was notorious for insisting on making his first appearance in an opera 'descending a hill on horseback and wearing a helmet with multi-coloured plumes at least a yard high' (Angus Heriot, *The Castrati in Opera*, London 1956, p.76). The castrato voice is sometimes thought to epitomise the artificiality of *opera seria*, in which castrati were customarily cast in the leading male roles. It is therefore salutary to be reminded that they were not all monsters of vanity; that such singers as Farinelli, perhaps the greatest of them all, and Gaetano Guadagni, Gluck's first Orfeo, could be men of humility, sincerity and genuine artistic dedication.

[45] The poet Thomas Gray, who was equally critical of the fashionable Italian opera of the day, suggested in a letter to Algarotti that not even Frederick the Great, Algarotti's patron, 'could govern an Italian *virtuosa*, destroy her caprice and impertinence, without hurting her talents, or command those unmeaning graces and tricks of voice to be silent that have gained her the adoration of her own country' (quoted in Edward J. Dent, *The Rise of Romantic Opera*, ed. Winton Dean, Cambridge 1976, pp.26f.). Gray in the same letter believes that it was a lack of literary education in those responsible for the production of operas that prevented the 'happy union' of music and drama that Algarotti proposed, but see chapter 1 of the essay for the latter's description of the ideal librettist.

Where shall we now find a man qualified to undertake the direction of an opera? In former times an aedile or an archon[46] did not think it beneath his rank to preside over theatrical exhibitions; and then each article was conducted with a suitable decorum, but more especially whenever the most celebrated of the ancient republics made a political use of scenic representations to arouse their citizens to a sense of glory, or to keep them peaceably diverted for the general quiet of the commonwealth.

But nowadays the fallen theatre, alas, groans under the mismanagement of mercenary and interested undertakers whose only object is to raise pecuniary contributions on the curiosity and leisure of their fellow citizens, they being for the most part totally unfit for such an employment through their gross ignorance of the several views proper to be conceived, or of the executive means to which they should have recourse in order that the desired effect may be obtained.

It is therefore necessary that an entire change in the manner of proceeding and a thorough reformation of those habitual errors be made, that a salutary doctrine, agreeable to the wishes of taste, may be adopted. Yet so praiseworthy a revolution can hardly be hoped for but under the patronage of a sovereign whose court affords a fostering asylum to the Muses; because there no man will dare to offer himself to be the director of such an entertainment but one duly qualified, and whose disposition to excel will go hand in hand with the means that shall be furnished to him. Under such a guidance, and never otherwise, shall we see the performers reduced to proper order and discipline; or we in consequence become spectators of dramatic compositions not inferior to those exhibited at Athens and Rome in the time of a Caesar and a Pericles.

---

[46] Magistrates in ancient Athens (the archon) and Rome (the aedile) responsible for public works and entertainments.

CHAPTER I

OF THE POEM, ARGUMENT OR BUSINESS OF AN OPERA

AS soon as the desired regulation shall have been introduced on the theatre it will then be incumbent to proceed to the various constituent parts of an opera, in order that those amendments should be made in each whereof they severally now appear the most deficient. The leading object to be maturely considered is the nature of the subject to be chosen - an article of much more consequence than is commonly imagined; for the success or failure of the drama depends in a great measure on a good or bad choice of the subject. It is here of no less consequence than in architecture the plan is to an edifice, or the canvas in painting is to a picture, because thereon the poet draws the outlines of his intended representation and its colouring is the task of the musical composer.[47] It is therefore the poet's duty, as chief engineer of the undertaking, to give directions to the dancers, the machinists, the painters: nay down even to those who are entrusted with the care of the wardrobe and dressing the performers. The poet is to carry in his mind a comprehensive view of the *whole* of the drama;[48] because those parts which are the productions of his pen ought to flow from the dictates of his actuating judgment which is to give being and movement to the whole.

At the first institution of operas the poets imagined the heathen mythology to be the best source from which they could derive subjects for their dramas. Hence *Daphne, Euridice, Ariana* were made choice of by Octavius Rinuccini and are

---

[47] Cf. the preface to *Alceste*, 'I thought <music> should act in the same way as an accurate and well executed drawing is brought to life by colour and by the well chosen contrast of light and shade, which serve to animate the figures without changing their shapes' (Patricia Howard, *op. cit.*, p.84).

[48] In an insightful essay on *Gluck and Reform Opera* accompanying the 1970 Decca recording conducted by Solti of *Orfeo ed Euridice* (SET.443/4) Arthur Hutchings refers to Winckelmann's celebrated definition of the essential qualities of classical art as enshrining 'an ideal which ... could be manifested only when *the part was subordinate to the whole* and distracting detail was suppressed for a "suprapersonal" proportion, so that a work *as a whole* seemed to be in magnificent repose.' As he also says, 'that is precisely the effect of the best reform operas.'

looked upon as the eldest musical dramas, having been exhibited about the beginning of the last century. There was besides Poliziano's *Orpheus,* which also had been represented with instrumental accompaniments, as well as another performance that was no more than a medley of dancing and music contrived by Bergonzo Botta for the entertainment of a duke of Milan in the city of Tortona. A particular species of drama was exhibited at Venice for the amusement of Henry the Third; it had been set to music by the famous Zarlino.[49] Add to these some other performances which ought only to be considered as so many rough sketches and preludes to a complete opera.

The intent of our poets was to revive the Greek tragedy in all its lustre and to introduce Melpomene on our stage, attended by music, dancing and all that imperial pomp with which at the brilliant periods of a Sophocles and Euripides she was wont to be escorted. And that such splendid pageantry might appear to be the genuine right of tragedy the poets had recourse for their subjects to the heroic ages and heathen mythology. From that fountain the bard, according to his inventive pleasure, introduced on the theatre all the deities of paganism, now shifting his scene to Olympus, now fixing it in the Elysian shades, now plunging it down to Tartarus with as much ease as if to Argos or to Thebes. And thus by the intervention of superior beings he gave an air of probability to most surprising and wonderful events. Every circumstance being thus elevated above the sphere of mortal existence, it necessarily followed that the singing of actors in an opera appeared a true imitation of the language made use of by the deities they represented.

---

[49] Ottavio Rinuccini wrote the libretti for three of the earliest operas: *Dafne* with music by Peri and *Euridice* with music by Peri and Caccini, both of 1600, and *Arianna* of 1608 with music by Monteverdi, of which only the celebrated lament survives. Poliziano's *Orfeo* of 1475 is said to be the first play to be written in the Italian language and may have been half spoken and half sung in performance, but there is no trace today of any musical setting. Jean-Philippe Navarre, in his edition of Algarotti's essay (*op. cit.*, p.99), suggests that the work by Bergonzo Botta was *La festa del paradiso,* presented at Milan in 1490 in celebration of a ducal wedding, while the Venice production may have been *La tragedia* of 1574 by Cornelio Frangipane, for which the music was by Claudio Merulo rather than Gioseffo Zarlino.

This then was the original cause why in the first dramas that had been exhibited in the courts of sovereigns or the palaces of princes, in order to celebrate their nuptials, such expensive machinery was employed; not an article was omitted that could excite an idea of whatever is most wonderful to be seen either on earth or in the heavens. To superadd a greater diversity, and thereby give a new animation to the whole, crowded choruses of singers were admitted, as well as dances of various contrivance, with a special attention that the execution of the ballet should coincide and be combined with the choral song: all which pleasing effects were made to spring naturally from the subject of the drama.

No doubt then can remain of the exquisite delight that such magic representations must have given to an enraptured assembly; for although it consisted but of a single subject, it nevertheless displayed an almost infinite variety of entertainment. There is even now frequent opportunity of seeing on the French musical theatre a spirited likeness to what is here advanced, because the opera was first introduced in Paris by Cardinal Mazarin, whither it carried the same magnificent apparatus with which it had made its appearance at his time in Italy.[50]

These representations must, however, have afterwards suffered not a little by the intermixture of buffoon characters, which are such ill-suited companions of the dignity of heroes and of gods; for by making the spectators laugh out of season they disconcert the solemnity of the piece. Some traces of this theatric impropriety are even now observable in the eldest of the French musical dramas.

The opera did not long remain confined in the courts of sovereigns and palaces of princes, but emancipating itself from such thraldom displayed its charms on public theatres to which the curious of all ranks were admitted for pay. But in this

---

[50] The Italian-born Mazarin had tried, partly for political reasons, to introduce Italian opera to Paris (see Michael F. Robinson, *Opera before Mozart*, London 1966, pp.26f.). On his death in 1661 King Louis XIV appointed as court composer his own favourite musician, Jean-Baptiste Lully, who was then able to develop the *tragédie lyrique* as much the same combination of the arts of music, dancing and stage spectacle as Algarotti approves here. There is admittedly also sometimes the admixture of comic elements that he deplores, e.g. the burlesque treatment of Charon in Lully's *Alceste* of 1674, though these did not long survive in Lully's work.

situation, as must obviously occur to whoever reflects, it was impossible that the pomp and splendour which was attendant on this entertainment from its origin could be continued. The falling off in that article was occasioned principally by the exorbitant salaries the singers insisted on, which had been but inconsiderable at the first outset of the musical drama; as for instance a certain female singer[51] was called *La Centoventi* (The Hundred-and-Twenty) for having received so many crowns for her performance during a single carnival - a sum which hath been amazingly exceeded since, almost beyond all bound.

Hence arose the necessity for opera directors to change their measures and to be as frugally economical on one hand as they found themselves unavoidably profuse on the other. Through such saving the opera may be said to have fallen from heaven upon the earth and, being divorced from an intercourse with gods, to have humbly resigned itself to that of mortals.

Thenceforward prevailed a general renunciation of all subjects to be found in the fabulous accounts of the heathen deities, and none were made choice of but those derived from the histories of humble mankind, because less magnificent in their nature and therefore less liable to large disbursements for their exhibition.

The directors, obliged to circumspection for their own safety, were induced to imagine that they might supply the place of all that costly pomp and splendid variety of decoration to which the dazzled spectators had been accustomed so long by introducing a chaster regularity into their drama, seconded by the auxiliary charms of a more poetical diction, as well as by the concurring powers of a more exquisite musical composition. This project gained ground the faster from the public's observing that one of these arts was entirely employed in modelling itself on our ancient authors; and the other solely intent on enriching itself with new ornaments, which made operas to be looked upon by many as having nearly

---

[51] Maria Maddalena Musi (1669-1751), one of the most admired and highest paid operatic singers of her day. For some years she was in the service of the Duke of Mantua, receiving an annual salary, a passport (something of a necessity for a theatrical career in the days of multiple small Italians states) and the designation *virtuosa*. At the height of her fame her appearances in Naples commanded a salary of 500 Spanish doubloons. She was also known as *La mignatta* (the leech), though this may be a name inherited from her mother, Lucrezia Mignati.

reached the pinnacle of perfection. However, that these representations might not appear too naked and uniform, interludes and ballets to amuse the audience were introduced between the acts; and thus by degrees the opera took that form which is now practised on our theatres.

It is an uncontrovertible fact that subjects for an operatical drama, whether taken from pagan mythology or historians, have inevitable inconveniences annexed to them. The fabulous subjects, on account of the great number of machines and magnificent apparatus which they require, often distress the poets into limits too narrow for him to carry on and unravel his plot with propriety; because he is not allowed either sufficient time or space to display the passions of each character, so absolutely necessary to the completing of an opera, which in the main is nothing more than a tragic poem recited to musical sounds; and from the inconvenience alluded to here it has happened that a great number of the French operas, as well as the first of the Italian, are nothing better than entertainments for the eyes, having more the appearance of a masquerade than of a regular dramatic performance: because therein the principal action is whelmed, as it were, under a heap of accessories, and the poetical part, being so flimsy and wretched, it was with just reason called a string of madrigals.

On the other hand the subjects taken from history are liable to the objection of their not being so well adapted to music, which seems to exclude them from all plea of probability. This impleaded error may be observed every day upon the Italian stage, for who can be brought to think that the trillings of an air flow so justifiably from the mouth of a Julius Caesar or a Cato as from the lips of Venus or Apollo? Moreover historical subjects do not furnish so striking a variety as those that are fabulous; they are apt to be too austere and monotonous. The stage in such representations would for ever exhibit an almost solitary scene, unless we are willing to number among the ranks of actors the mob of attendants that crowd after sovereigns, even into their closets. Besides it is no easy matter to contrive ballets or interludes suitable to subjects taken from history; because all such entertainments ought to form a kind of social union and become, as it were, constituent parts of the whole. Such, for example, on the French stage is *The Ballet of the Shepherds* that celebrates the marriage of Medoro with Angelica and makes Orlando acquainted with his accumulated wretchedness.[52] But this is far from being the effect of entertainments obtruded into the Italian operas in which, although the subject be Roman and the ballet consist of dancers dressed like Roman soldiers, yet so unconnected is it with the business of the drama that the scozzese or furlana might as well be danced. And this is the reason why subjects chosen from history are for the most part necessitated to appear naked, or to make use of such alien accoutrements as neither belong nor are by any means suitable to them.

In order to obviate such inconveniences the only means left to the poet is to exert all his judgment and taste in choosing the subject of his drama that thereby he may attain his end, which is to delight the eyes and the ears, to rouse up and to affect the hearts of an audience without the risk of sinning against reason or commonsense: wherefore the most prudent method he can adopt will be to make choice of an event that has happened either in very remote times or in countries very distant from us and quite estranged from our usages, which may afford various incidents of the marvellous, notwithstanding that the subject at the same time be extremely simple and not unknown: two desirable requisites.

The great distance of place where the action is fixed will prevent the recital of it to musical sounds from appearing quite so improbable to us. The marvellousness of the theme will furnish the author with an opportunity of interweaving therewith dances, choruses and a variety of scenical decorations. The simplicity and notoriety of it will exempt his Muse from the perplexing trouble and tedious preparations necessary to make personages of a drama known that, suitable to his notification, may be displayed their passions, the mainspring and actuating spirit of the stage.[53]

---

[52] In Act 4 of Lully's *Roland* of 1685, a scene particularly admired in the 18th century for its integrated dramatic use of the danced divertissement.

[53] For a discussion of verisimilitude in the choice of subjects for opera see Hamish F. G. Swanston, *In Defence of Opera*, London 1978, chapter 2, 'Is it for real?' especially pp.66-73.

The two operas of Dido and of Achilles in Scyros, written by the celebrated Metastasio, come very near to the mark proposed here.[54] The subjects of these dramatic poems are simple and taken from very remote antiquity, but without being too far fetched. In the midst of their most impassioned scenes there is an opportunity of introducing splendid banquets, magnificent embassies, embarkations, choruses, battles, conflagrations etc., so as to give a further extension to the sovereignty of the musical drama and make its rightfulness be more ascertained than has been hitherto allowed.

The same doctrine may be advanced in regard to an opera on the subject of Montezuma, as much on account of the greatness as of the novelty of such an action as that emperor's catastrophe must afford. A display of the Mexican and Spanish customs, seen for a first time together, must form a most beautiful contrast; and the barbaric magnificence of America would receive heightenings by being opposed in different views to that of Europe.[55]

Several subjects may likewise be taken from Ariosto and Tasso,[56] equally fitting as Montezuma for the opera theatre, for besides these being so universally known, they would furnish not only a fine field for exercising the passions, but also for introducing all the surprising illusions of the magic art.

An opera of Aeneas in Troy or Iphigenia in Aulis would answer the same purpose,[57] and to the great variety for scenes and machinery still greater heightenings might be derived from the enchanting *poetry* of Virgil and Euripides.

There are many other subjects to the full as applicable to the stage and that may be found equally fraught with marvellous incidents. Let then a poet who is judicious enough make a prudent collection of the subjects truly dramatic that are

---

[54] Libretti of 1724 and 1736 respectively, both texts set several times by different composers.

[55] [Author's note:] Montezuma has been chosen for the subject of an opera performed with the greatest magnificence at the theatre royal of Berlin [libretto (written in French, but sung in Italian translation) by Frederick the Great, music by Carl Heinrich Graun, first performed 6 January 1755].

[56] The 16th century Italian epics, *Orlando furioso* by Ariosto and *La Gerusalemme liberata* of Tasso, were the source of operas such as Handel's *Orlando* and Lully's and Gluck's *Armide*. For Handel's use of Ariosto see Gary Schmidgall, *Literature as Opera*, New York 1977, pp.46-57.

[57] Algarotti offers his own versions of these two scenarios in the appendix to his essay.

to be found in tracing the fabulous accounts of the heathen gods and do the same also in regard to more modern times. Such a proceeding relative to the opera would not be unlike to what is oft times necessary in states which it is impossible to preserve from decay and in the unimpaired enjoyment of constitutional vigour without making them revert from time to time to their original principles.

CHAPTER II

OF THE MUSICAL COMPOSITION FOR OPERAS

NO art now appears to stand so much in need of having the conclusive maxim of the preceding chapter put in practice as that of music, so greatly has it degenerated from its former dignity. For by laying aside every regard to decorum and by scorning to keep within the bound prescribed it has suffered itself to be led far, very far astray in a bewildered pursuit of new-fangled whimsies and capricious conceits. Wherefore it would be now very seasonable to revive the decree made by the Lacedaemonians[58] against that man who through a distempered passion for novelty had so sophisticated their music with his crotchety inventions that from noble and manly he rendered it effeminate and disgusting.

Mankind in general, it must be owned, are actuated by a love of novelty, and it is as true that without it music, like every other art, could not have received the great improvements it has. What we here implead is not a chaste passion for novelty, but a too great fondness for it; because it was that which reduced music to the declining state so much lamented by all true connoisseurs. While arts are in their infancy the love of novelty is no doubt essential, as it is to that they owe their being, and after by its kindly influence are improved, matured and brought to perfection; but that point being once attained, the indulging this passion too far will, from benign and vivifying, become noxious and fatal. The arts have experienced this vicissitude in almost every nation where they have appeared: as among the Italians hath music at this time in a more remarkable manner.

---

[58] The ancient Spartans, who according to Boethius (*De institutione musica*, i.1) passed a decree expelling from their city the poet and musician Timotheus of Miletus, a pioneer of the so-called "new music" who reacted against the classical Greek style at the end of the 5th century B.C. His transgression was to add an extra string (or strings – accounts differ) to the cithara, a harp-like instrument of the lyre family sacred to Apollo, thus enabling his music to become more varied and capricious. The authenticity of the decree is now considered doubtful, but the Spartans' objections to Timotheus are mentioned by other ancient authors: Pausanias, for example (*Description of Greece* iii.12.10), says that the Spartans hung Timotheus' harp in the meeting-house of their Assembly to express their disapproval of his having added four strings to its original seven.

On its revival in Italy, though in very barbarous times, this elegant art soon made its power be known throughout Europe; nay more, it was cultivated to such a degree by the tramontane nations that it may without exaggeration be asserted, the Italians themselves were for a certain period of time glad to receive instructions from them.

On the return of music to Venice, Rome, Bologna and Naples, as to its native place, such considerable improvements were made there in the musical art during the two last centuries that foreigners in their turn repaired thither for instruction: and such would be now the case, were they not deterred from so doing by the raging frenzy after novelty that prevails in all the Italian schools. For as if music were yet unrudimented and in its infancy, the mistaken professors spare no pains to trick out their art with every species of grotesque imagination and fantastical combination which they think can be executed by sounds. The public too, as if they were likewise in a state of childhood, change almost every moment their notions of and fondness for things, rejecting today with scorn what yesterday was so passionately admired. The taste in singing, which some years ago enraptured audiences hung upon with wonder and delight, is now received with a supercilious disapprobation: not because it is sunk in real merit, but for the very groundless reason of its being old and not in frequent use. And thus we see that in compositions instituted for the representation of nature, whose mode is ever one, there is the same desire of changing as in the fluctuating fashions of the dresses we wear.

Another principal reason that can be assigned for the present degeneracy of music is the authority, power and supreme command usurped in its name, because the composer in consequence acts like a despotic sovereign, contracting all the views of pleasing to his department alone. It is almost impossible to persuade him that he ought to be in a subordinate station, that music derives its greatest merit from being no more than an auxiliary, the handmaid to poetry. His chief business then is to predispose the minds of the audience for receiving the impression to be excited by the poet's verse; to infuse such a general tendency in their affections as

19

to make them analogous with those particular ideas which the poets mean to inspire. In fine, its genuine office is to communicate a more animating energy to the language of the Muses.[59]

That old and just charge, enforced by critics against operatical performances, of making their heroes and heroines die *singing* can be ascribed to no other cause but the defect of a proper harmony between the words and the music. Were all ridiculous quavering omitted when the serious passions are to speak, and were the musical composition judiciously adapted to them, then it would not appear more improbable that a person should die singing than reciting verses.

It is an undeniable fact that in the earliest ages the poets were all musical proficients; the vocal part then ranked as it should, which was to render the thoughts of the mind and affections of the heart with more forcible, more lively and more kindling expression. But now that the twin sisters, poetry and music, go no longer hand in hand, it is not at all surprising if the business of the one is to add colouring to what the other has designed, that the colouring, separately considered, appear beautiful; yet, upon a nice examination of the whole, the contours offend by not being properly rounded and by the absence of a social blending of the parts throughout. Nor can a remedy be applied to so great an evil otherwise than by the modest discretion of a composer who will not think it beneath him to receive from the poet's mouth the purport of his meaning and intention, who will also make himself a competent master of the author's sense before he writes a note of music, and will ever afterwards confer with him

---

[59] [Author's note 1764:] 'If Painting be inferior to Poetry, Music, considered as an imitative art, must be greatly inferior to Painting: for as Music has no means of explaining the motives of its various impressions, its imitations of the Manners and Passions must be extremely vague and undecisive: for instance, the tender and melting tones which may be expressive of the Passion of Love, will be equally in unison with the collateral feelings of Benevolence, Friendship, Pity and the like. Again, how are we to distinguish the rapid movements of Anger from those of Terror, Distraction and all the violent agitations of the Soul? But let Poetry co-operate with Music and specify the motive of each particular impression, we are no longer at a loss: we acknowledge the agreement of the sound with the idea and general impressions become specific indications of the Manners and the Passions' – *Remarks on the beauties of Poetry*, by Daniel Webb Esq., p.102 in the note. [Daniel Webb (c.1719-1798) wrote three important treatises on aesthetics: *Remarks on the beauties of Poetry* dates from 1762; the others are on painting and the correspondences between poetry and music.]

concerning the music he shall have composed; and by thus proceeding keep up such a dependence and friendly intercourse as subsisted between Lully and Quinault, Vinci and Metastasio,[60] which indeed the true regulation of an operatical theatre requires.

Among the errors observable in the present system of music the most obvious, and that which first strikes the ears at the very opening of an opera, is the hackneyed manner of composing overtures, which are always made to consist of two allegros with one grave, and to be as noisy as possible. Thus they are void of variation and so jog on much alike. Yet what a wide difference ought to be perceived between that, for example, which precedes the death of Dido and that which is prefixed to the nuptials of Demetrius and Cleonice.[61] The main drift of an overture should be to announce in a certain manner the business of the drama, and consequently prepare the audience to receive those affecting impressions that are to result from the whole of the performance; so that from hence a leading view and presaging notions of it may be conceived as is of an oration from the exordium.[62] But our present composers look upon an overture as an article quite detached and absolutely different from the poet's drama. They use it as an opportunity of playing off a tempestuous music to stun the ears of an audience. If some, however, employ it as an exordium, it is of a kindred complexion to those of certain writers who with big and pompous words repeatedly display before us the loftiness of the subject and the lowness of their genius; which preluding would

---

[60] Two of the most celebrated composer-librettist partnerships in Baroque opera, though many of Metastasio's libretti were set several times over by different composers. As one of the two principal authors of *opera seria* his work used to be maligned: for a juster appraisal see Patrick J. Smith, *The Tenth Muse: A Historical Study of the Opera Libretto*, New York 1970, ch. 6. Metastasio's intention in *opera seria,* as shown in his advice to the composer Hasse quoted by Smith, e.g. in matters of orchestration and treatment of the recitative, was the creation of a true musical *drama*. In this connection it is instructive that even after the reform of *Orfeo ed Euridice* Gluck did not disdain to set libretti by Metastasio, such as *Il trionfo di Clelia* the very next year.

[61] *Demetrio,* otherwise known as *Cleonice,* was a libretto of Metastasio set, among others, by Gluck in 1742.

[62] Cf. the preface to *Alceste:* 'I considered that the sinfonia [i.e. overture] should inform the spectators of the subject that is to be enacted and constitute, as it were, the argument' (in Patricia Howard, *Gluck: an 18th Century Portrait in Letters and Documents,* Oxford 1995, p.85). The overture to *Alceste* itself is the first by Gluck of which this holds true: *Orfeo ed Euridice* has a conventional festive 18th century opera overture bearing little connection with the ensuing scene.

suit any other subject as well and might as judiciously be prefixed for an exordium to one oration as another.

After the overture the next article that presents itself to our consideration is the recitative; and as it is wont to be the most noisy part of an opera,[63] so is it the least attended to and the most neglected. It seems as if our musical composers were of opinion that the recitative is not of consequence enough to deserve their attention, they deeming it incapable of exciting any great delight. But the ancient masters thought in quite a different manner. There needs no stronger proof than to read what Jacopo Peri, who may be justly called the inventor of the recitative, wrote in his preface to *Euridice*. When he had applied himself to an investigation of that species of musical imitation which would the readiest lend itself to theatric exhibitions, he directed his tasteful researches to discover the manner which had been employed by the ancient Greeks on similar occasions. He carefully observed the Italian words which are capable of intonation or consonance and those which are not. He was very exact in minuting down our several modes of pronunciation, as well as the different accents of grief, of joy and of all the other affections incident to the human frame; and that in order to make the bass move a timing attendance to them, now with more energy, now with less, according to the nature of each. So nicely scrupulous was he in his course of vocal experiments that he scrutinized intimately the very genius of the Italian language; on which account, in order to be more accurate, he frequently consulted with several gentlemen not less remarkable for the delicacy of their ears than for their being uncommonly skilled both in the arts of music and of poetry.[64]

---

[63] *Strepitosa* is the word translated 'noisy.' It seems a strange description to modern ears, considering that so much of the recitative in *opera seria* is of the *secco* variety, accompanied only by a harpsichord. Perhaps Algarotti means that audiences often paid it little attention, talking and chatting instead and so making much noise of their own!

[64] Algarotti clearly made a careful study of Peri's preface, if not of his music. According to John D. Drummond 'it is doubtful whether Algarotti actually knew any of the early Baroque operas, but his text makes it clear that he knew of them by name and had a good idea of what their composers were trying to achieve' (*Opera in Perspective,* London 1980, p.359, footnote 8 to ch. 5). An English translation of Peri's text may be found in *Source Readings in Musical History: from Classical Antiquity to the Romantic Era,* selected and annotated by Oliver Strunk, London 1952, pp.373-376.

The final conclusion of his ingenious enquiry was that the ground-work of all such imitation should be an harmony, chastely following nature step by step; a something between common speaking and melody; a well-combined sytem between that kind of performance which the ancients called the *diastematica,* as if held in and suspended; and the other called the *continuata*.[65] Such were the studies of the musical composers in former times. They proceeded in the improvement of their art with the utmost care and attention; and the effect proved that they did not lose their time in the pursuit of unprofitable subtleties.

The recitative in their time was made to vary with the subject and assume a complexion suitable to the spirit of the words. It sometimes moved with a rapidity equal to that of the text and at others with an attendant slowness, but never failed to mark in a conspicuous manner those inflexions and sallies which the violence of our passions can transfuse into the expression of them. All musical compositions finished in so masterly a manner were heard with delight. Numbers now living must remember how certain passages of simple recitative have affected the minds of an audience to a degree that no modern air is able to produce.

However, the recitative, all disregarded as it may be, has been known to excite emotion in an audience when it was of the *obligato* kind, as the artists term it, that is, when strictly accompanied with instruments. Perhaps it would not be improper to employ it oftener than is now the custom. What a kindly warmth might be communicated to the recitative if, where a passion exerts itself, it were to be enforced by the united orchestra![66] By so doing the heart and mind at once would be stormed, as it were, by all the powers of music. A more evincing instance of such an effect cannot be quoted than the greater part of the last act of *Didone* set

---

[65] For these two terms see the glossary at the end.
[66] Cf. the preface to *Alceste:* '<I considered that> the ensemble of instruments should be formed with reference to the interest and feeling, without leaving that sharp division in the dialogue between aria and recitative' (in Patricia Howard, *op.cit.*, p.85). The recitative in *Orfeo ed Euridice* is orchestrally accompanied throughout: in *Alceste,* his second reform opera, Gluck strangely reverted to *secco.*

to music by Vinci,[67] which is executed in the taste recommended here: and no doubt but Virgil's self would be pleased to hear a composition so animating and so terrible.

Another good purpose which must be derived from such a practice is that then would not appear to us so enormous the great variety and disproportion now observable in the *andamento* of the recitative and that of the airs; but on the contrary a more friendly agreement among the several parts of an opera would be the result. The connoisseurs have been often displeased with those sudden transitions where, from a recitative in the *andantissimo* and gentlest movement, the performers are made to skip off and bound away into *ariettas* of the briskest execution; which is to the full as absurd as if a person, when soberly walking, should all on the sudden set to leaping and capering.

The surest method to bring about a better understanding among the several constituent parts of an opera would be not to crowd so much art into the airs and to curb the instrumental part more than is now the custom. In every period of the opera these two formed the most brilliant parts of it: and in proportion as the musical composition has been more and more refined, so have they received still greater heightenings. They were naked formerly in comparison of what we see them now, and were in as absolute a state of simplicity as they had been at their origin, insomuch that either in point of melody or accompaniments they did not rise above recitative.

Old Scarlatti[68] was the first who infused life, movement and spirit in them. It was he who clothed their nakedness with the splendid attire of noble accompaniments; but they were dealt out by him in a sober and judicious manner. They were by no means intricate or obscure, but open and obvious, highly finished, yet free from all the minuteness of affectation; and that not so much on

---

[67] The musical score of this scene, a departure from Vinci's customary simple style of recitative, is included as an appendix to Jean-Philippe Navarre's edition of Algarotti's essay: *op. cit.*, pp.240-247.

[68] Alessandro Scarlatti (1660-1725), the foremost Italian opera composer of his generation and musical founder of Neapolitan *opera seria*, father of the celebrated harpsichordist and composer Domenico who also wrote operas.

account of the vastness of the theatres, by means of which many of the minor excellencies in musical performances may be lost, as in regard to the voices to which alone they should be made subservient.

But unwarrantable changes have happened since that great master's time down to ours in which all the bounds of discretion are wantonly overleapt. The airs now are whelmed under and disfigured by crowded ornaments with which unnatural method the rage of novelty labours to embellish them. How tediously prolix are those *ritornelli* that precede them; nay, and are often superfluous. For can anything be more improbable than that in an air expressive of wrath an actor should calmly wait with his hand stuck in his sword-belt until the ritornello be over, to give vent to a passion that is supposed to be boiling in his breast?[69] and after the ritornello then comes on the part to be sung, but the multitude of fiddles etc. that accompany it in general produce no better an effect than to astonish the faculty of hearing and to drown the voice of a singer. Why is there not more use made of the basses, and why not increase the number of bass viols, which are the shades of music? Where is the necessity for so many fiddles, with which our orchestras are now thronged? Fewer would do; for they prove in this case like too many hands on board of a ship, which instead of being assistant are a great impediment to its navigation. Why are not lutes and harps allowed a place? with their light and piercing notes they would give a sprightliness to the *ripienos*. Why is the *violetta*[70] excluded from our orchestras, since from its institution it was intended to act a middle part between the fiddles and the basses in order that harmony might thence ensue?

But one of the most favourite practices now, and which indeed makes our theatres to resound with peals of applause, is in an *air* to form a contest between the voice and a hautboy or between the voice and a trumpet, so as to exhibit, as it

---

[69] Cf. the preface to *Alceste:* 'I did not ... want to hold up an actor in the white heat of dialogue to wait for a tedious *ritornello* ' (in Patricia Howard, *op. cit.,* p.84).

[70] *Pace* the note in the glossary Algarotti seems to indicate here the viola.

were, a kind of musical tilting match with the utmost exertion on either side.[71] But such a skirmishing of voices and instruments is very displeasing to the judicious part of an audience who, on the contrary, would receive the greatest delight from the airs being accompanied by instruments differently qualified from the present in use, and perhaps even by the organ, as hath been formerly practised.[72] The consequence then would be that the respective qualities of instruments would be properly adapted to the nature of the words which they are intended to accompany, and that they would aptly glide into those parts where a due expression of the passion should stand most in need of them. Then the accompaniment would be of service to the singer's voice by enforcing the pathetic affections of the song; and would prove not unlike to the numbers of elegant and harmonious prose which, according to the maxim of a learned sage, ought to be like the beating on an anvil by smiths, at once both musical and skilfully laboured.

These faults, however considerable, are not the greatest that have been introduced in the composition of airs; we must go farther back to investigate the first source of this evil, which, in the judgment of the most able professors, is to be found in the misconduct of choosing the subject of an air: because rarely any attention is paid to the andamento of the melody being natural and corresponding to the sense of the words it is to convey; besides, the extravagant varieties which it is now made to shift and turn about after cannot be managed to tend to one common centre or point of unity. For the chief view of our present musical composers is to court, flatter and surprise the ears, but not at all either to affect the heart or kindle the imagination of those who hear them; wherefore, to accomplish their favourite end they frequently bound over all rules. To be prodigal of shining passages, to repeat words without end and musically to interweave or entangle them as they please are the three principal methods by which they carry on their operations.

---

[71] Dr. Burney records just such a contest between the celebrated Farinelli and a trumpeter occurring each night during the run of an opera in Rome: see Heriot, *op. cit.*, pp.96f.

[72] [Author's Note:] In the *orchestra* of the theatre in the famous city of Cataio an organ is now to be seen. [Cattajo is a 16th century villa with fine gardens at Battaglia Terme near Padua.]

The first of these expedients is indeed big with danger when we attend to the good effect that is to be expected from melody, because through its middle situation it possesses more of the *virtù*. Moreover, music delights to make an use of acute notes in her compositions similar to that which painting does with striking lights in her performances.

In regard to brilliant passages, common sense forbids the introduction of them excepting where the words are expressive of passion or movement, otherwise they deserve no milder an appellation than being so many impertinent interruptions of the musical sense.[73]

The repeating of words and these chiming rencounters that are made for the sake of sound merely and are devoid of meaning prove intolerable to a judicious ear. Words are to be treated in no other manner but according as the passion dictates: and when the sense of an air is finished the first part of it ought never to be sung over again; which is one of our modern innovations and quite repugnant to the natural process of our speech and passions, that are not accustomed to thus turn about and recoil upon themselves.[74] Most people who frequent our Italian theatres must have observed that even when the sense of an air breathes a roused and furious tendency, yet if the words Father or Son be in the text the composer never fails to slacken his notes, to give all the softness he can and to stop in a moment the impetuosity of the tune. Moreover he flatters himself on such occasion that, besides having clothed the words with sentimental sounds suitable to them, he hath also given to them an additional seasoning of variety.

---

[73] Cf. Gluck writing to the *Mercure de France* 1 February 1773: 'The imitation of nature is the acknowledged end at which all must aim. It is the one I endeavour to attain. Always as simple and natural as possible, my music aspires only to achieve the fullest expression and to follow the declamation of the poetry. This is why I never use trills, passage-work, or cadenzas which the Italians employ in profusion' (in Patricia Howard, *op. cit.*, p.106)

[74] Cf. the preface to *Alceste*: 'I did not feel it my duty to skim quickly over the second part of an aria, which may well contain the most passionate and significant words, in order to have space to repeat exactly, four times over, the words of the first part, or to accommodate a singer who wants to show in how many ways he can capriciously vary a passage, rather than ending the aria where its meaning ends' (*ibid.*, p.84).

But in our sense he hath entirely spoiled all with such a dissonance of expression that will ever be objected to by all who have the least pretensions to judgment and taste. The duty of a composer is to express the sense, not of this or that particular word, but the comprehensive meaning of all the words in the air. It is also his duty to make variety flow from the several modifications the subject in itself is capable of; and not from adjuncts that adventitiously fasten themselves thereon and are foreign from, preposterous or repugnant to the poet's intention.

It seems that our composers take the same mistaken pains which some writers do; who, regardless of connection and order in a discourse, bent all their thoughts to collect and string together a number of finely sounding words. But notwithstanding such words are ever so harmonious, a discourse so written would prove an useless, vain and contemptible performance. The same may be said of every musical composition which is not calculated either to express some sentiment or awaken the idea of some imagery of the mind.[75] Like what we have

---

[75] [Author's note:] '*Toute musique qui ne peint rien n'est que du bruit, et sans l'habitude, qui dénature tout, elle ne ferait guère plus de plaisir qu'une suite de mots harmonieux et sonores, dénués de l'ordre et de liaison*' (*Préface de l'Encyclopédie*). All music that paints nothing is only noise, and were it not for custom, that unnatures everything, it would excite no more pleasure than a sequel of harmonious and finely sounding words, without any order or connection.

[The 18th century lacked a developed independent aesthetic theory of music. Writers tended instead to assimilate their understanding of the nature of music to the prevailing Aristotelian representational theory of art in general and could sometimes belittle the expressive powers of music in comparison with painting and poetry, cf. the quotation from Daniel Webb in footnote 59 (Ernest Newman discusses several writers of the time in his *Gluck and the Opera: a Study in Musical History*, London 1895, Part II, chapter 3, pp.238-274). Algarotti is in accord with the accepted aesthetic in insisting throughout the essay that opera should be true to life.

He may also reflect the influence of the Classical treatise known as Longinus *On the Sublime*, which enjoyed great prestige in the 18th century: see e.g. Jean Benedetti, *David Garrick and the Birth of Modern Theatre*, London 2001, pp.26-8. Longinus' identification of poetic defects that detract from sublimity, such as over-inflation or frigidity, recall the criticisms of *opera seria* - the defects in both cases proceeding from the same source: 'that passion for novel ideas which is the dominant craze among the writers of today' (Longinus ch. 5 in *Classical Literary Criticism*, tr. and introd. T. S. Dorsch, London 1965, p.106) or 'distempered passion for novelty' (*stemperato amore della novità*) as Algarotti puts it at the beginning of this chapter.

Following the above quotation he adds in the 1764 version of the essay: 'Most felicitous is the saying of Fontenelle: *Sonate, que me veux-tu?* (Sonata, what do you want of me?) But he would probably not have said this of the sonatas of the incomparable Tartini, in which one finds the greatest variety combined with the most perfect unity. Before getting down to composition he was in the habit of reading a certain poem of Petrarch. He had much sympathy with its elegance of feeling, and that helped him to dispose himself to what was given him to depict, together with the various accompanying modifications, and not lose sight of the theme or the subject.']

compared it to it must turn out but an useless and a vain production, which, should it be received with a temporary and slight applause, must soon be consigned to perpetual silence and oblivion, notwithstanding all the art that might have been employed in choosing the musical combinations. On the contrary, those airs alone remain for ever engraven on the memory of the public that paint images in the mind, or express the passions, and are for that reason called the speaking airs,[76] because more congenial to nature; which can never be justly imitated, but by a beautiful simplicity,[77] which will always bear away the palm from the most laboured refinements of art.

Although poetry and music be so near akin to each other, yet they have pursued different views here in Italy. The music, presiding over harmony, was too chaste in the last century to give in to those affectations and languishing airs which she is at present so fond of indulging. She then knew the way to the human heart, and how to stamp permanent impressions thereon; she possessed the secret of incorporating herself, as it were, with the meaning of the words, and that the probability might seem the greater, she was to the last degree simple, yet affecting; though at the same time the poetic Muse had run away from all semblance of truth to make a parade of hyperbolical, far-fetched fantastical whimsies. Since that time, by a strange vicissitude, as soon as poetry was made to return into the right path music ran astray.

Such excellent masters as a Cesti and a Carissimi[78] had the hard fate of composing music for words in the style of the Achillino,[79] men who were equal to the noble task of conveying in musical numbers the sighs and love-breathings of a Petrarch. But now, alas! The elegant, the terse, the graceful poems of Metastasio

---

[76] The *aria parlante* was a recognised type in *opera seria* that relied more on vigour of expression than *bravura* or *coloratura* writing.

[77] *Bella semplicità* is of course the watchword both of D'Alembert's approach to art in the preface to the *Encyclopaedia* and of Gluck and Calzabigi in their reform style of opera.

[78] Antonio Cesti was a leading composer of operas of the mid 17th century, the generation following Monteverdi and Cavalli. His contemporary Giacomo Carissimi is known as one of the progenitors of the oratorio.

[79] Claudio Achillini (1574-1640) was a friend and supporter of Marini (see footnote 94), two of whose poems Monteverdi set as madrigals.

are degraded into music by wretched composers. It must not, however, be hence concluded that no vestige of true music is to be perceived among us; because, as a proof against such an opinion, and that no small one, may be produced our intermezzi and comic operas; wherein the first of all musical requisites, that of expression, takes the lead more than in any other of our compositions: which is owing perhaps to the impossibility the masters found of indulging their own fancy in a wanton display of all the secrets of their art and the manifold treasures of musical knowledge; from which ostentatious prodigality they were luckily prevented by the very limited abilities of their singers. Wherefore, in their own despite, they found themselves obliged to cultivate simplicity and follow nature. Whatever may have been the cause, this style soon obtained the vogue and triumphed over every other, although called plebeian. Why did it succeed? Because it was fraught with truth, that in all parts and sciences must ultimately prevail.

To this kind of performance we owe the extending of our musical fame on the other side of the Alps among the French, who had been at all times our rivals in every polite art. The emulous contention which had so long subsisted between them and us for a pre-eminence in music is universally known. No means could be hit on by our artists to make their execution agreeable to Gallic ears; and the Italian melody was abhorred by them as much as had been in former times an Italian regency.

But no sooner was heard upon the theatre of Paris the natural, yet elegant style of the *Serva Padrona,* rich with airs so expressive and duets so pleasing, than the far greater part of the French became not only proselytes to, but even zealous advocates in behalf of the Italian music. A revolution so sudden was caused by an intermezzo and two comic actors.[80] The like had been attempted in vain in the most elaborate pieces of eminent composers through a long series of years,

---

[80] *Buffoni.* There is a third, non-speaking part in Pergolesi's work, the production of which at Paris in 1752 sparked off the famous *querelle des bouffons*, the war of words between the rival partisans of French and Italian styles in music. The continuing dispute flared again into open conflagration with the conflict between Gluck and Piccinni, or at least their supporters, at Paris in 1777.

although bedizened over with so many brilliant passages, surprising shakes, etc. Nor did the repeated efforts of our most celebrated performers, vocal or instrumental, fare better.

Nevertheless, all the good musical composition modern Italy can boast of is not absolutely confined to the intermezzi and comic operas; for it must be confessed that in some of our late serious pieces there are parts not unworthy of the best masters and the most applauded era of music. Several instances are to be found in the works of Pergolesi and Vinci, whom death too soon snatched from us, as well as in those of Galuppi, Jommelli, Sassone,[81] that are deserving to be for ever in esteem.

Through the energy of the composition of these masters music makes an audience feel sometimes from the stage the very same effects that were formerly felt in the chapels under the direction of Palestrina and Rhodio.[82] We have likewise proofs of the like powerful influence in the skilful productions of Benedetto Marcello, a man second in merit to none among the ancients and certainly the first among the moderns. Who ever was more animated with a divine flame in conceiving and more judicious in conducting his works than Marcello? In

---

[81] Handel was known to the Italians as *il caro Sassone* (the dear Saxon), but in this context the sobriquet probably refers to his fellow-Saxon Johann Adolf Hasse (1699-1783), one of the most widely admired composers of *opere serie* in Italy and German-speaking countries during the first half of the 18th century. Similarly admired were the four Italians mentioned here, all these composers renowned for the dramatic quality of their operatic music. Pergolesi died at the age of 26 and Vinci at 34. One may note that Algarotti's estimation of composers changed over the years in which he worked on this essay: in the original 1755 version the favoured ones are Gasparini, Bononcini and Alessandro Scarlatti; his admiration for Marcello, however, remained constant.

[82] I.e. Rocco Rodio (1532-1616), composer of masses, madrigals and ricercars presaging the style of Frescobaldi, known also for his treatise on *The Rules of Music* of 1600. In the 1764 edition Algarotti removed the reference to Palestrina and Rodio and inserted a new passage on the appropriateness of counterpoint in dramatic music. He suggests that counterpoint may suitably lend grandeur and solemnity to church music, but since melody is the most apt for expressing human feeling counterpoint would need to be employed sparingly and with fine judgment in operatic composition: for the text see Jean-Philippe Navarre, *op. cit.*, pp.114f. Handel famously remarked that Gluck knew no more counterpoint than his cook, but Patricia Howard shows that 'Gluck's contrapuntal ability is a much maligned aspect of his technique' and that he recognised well how to use it judiciously for dramatic purposes - exactly as Algarotti proposes (see her *Gluck and the Birth of Modern Opera*, London 1963, pp.84f.).

the cantatas of Timoteo, of Cassandra and of the celebrated opera of Salmi[83] he hath expressed in a wonderful manner not only all the different passions of the heart, but even the most delicate sentiments of the mind. He has moreover the art of representing to our fancy things even inanimate. He found out the secret of associating with all the gracefulness and charms of the modern the chaste correctness of ancient music, which in him appears like the attractive graces of a beloved and respected matron.[84]

---

[83] Benedetto Marcello (1686-1739) was renowned for his collection of psalm-settings *Estro poetico-armonico* as well as for cantatas and oratorios. *Opera* in the Italian means simply 'works.' The translator may have misinterpreted *Salmi* as the title of an opera. Navarre's edition includes in an appendix the musical scores of Marcello's cantata *Timoteo,* referred to here, and his setting of Psalm 1: *op. cit.,* pp.248-314.

[84] [Author's note 1764:] 'The first of these is Benedetto Marcello, whose inimitable Freedom, Depth and comprehensive style will ever remain the highest Example to all Composers for the Church. For the service of which he published at Venice, near thirty years ago, the first fifty Psalms set to Music. Here he has far excelled all the Moderns and given us the truest Idea of that noble simplicity which probably was the grand Characteristic of the ancient Music. In this extensive and laborious undertaking, like the divine subject he works upon, he is generally either grand, beautiful or pathetic; and so perfectly free from every Thing that is low and common, that the judicious Hearer is charmed with an endless variety of new and pleasing Modulation, together with a Design and Expression so finely adapted that the sense and Harmony do everywhere coincide. In the last Psalm, which is the fifty-first in our Version, he seems to have collected all the Powers of his vast Genius, that he might surpass the Wonders he had done before.' - *An Essay on Musical Expression,* by Charles Avison, Organist in Newcastle [published at London in 1752. It was an early attempt at musical aesthetics that sought to describe the effects of music in ordinary rather than technical language].

CHAPTER III

OF THE RECITATIVE AND SINGING IN OPERAS

IT is not enough for correct musical composition in order to succeed that it be attentive to what effect it shall produce, because that depends chiefly on the manner in which it is executed by the singers. For it may so happen that a good musical composer may be a good commander at the head of a bad army, with this difference that a good commander may make good soldiers, but a skilful composer of music cannot flatter himself to do the like with his singers. It has never entered into the heads of most of them how necessary above every other article it is to learn an accurate pronunciation of their own language, to articulate well, to be intelligible and not to change, as is too often the case, one word for another. Nothing is more ungraceful than their mincing and frittering away the finales, as well as their clipping and mutilating words, lest they should offend their own tender palates; by which means those who have not the books of the drama open before them do not receive by their ears any distinct impression of what is unmeaningly lisped away. It was glancing at this error that Salvini[49] humorously remarked, 'Such acting, which to be understood labours under the inconvenience of its drama being read, is not unlike to those pictures under which it is necessary to write, this is a dog and this a horse.' To Italy, much better than to France, might be applied the pleasant caricature that was made there of an opera without words, as if in an opera words were quite superfluous.[50]

---

[49] Anton Maria Salvini (1653-1729), Classical scholar and member of the Florentine *Accademia della Crusca,* which helped to establish the purified Tuscan dialect as the literary language of Italy in the 16th and 17th centuries.

[50] [Author's note:] The amours of the emperor Caracalla with a vestal, by Le Grand. [This note appears in Algarotti's text in French. It has not been possible to trace the work referred to here. There was an opera *I due cesari* (The two Caesars) by Giovanni Legrenzi, presented at Venice in 1683, in which the Roman emperor Bassanius Caracalla is a leading character. The plot concerns his love for Onoria and his attempts to deprive his brother Geta of his share in the throne desired by their father, the former emperor Septimius Severus. A contemporary report suggested that the lack of stage spectacle in the production was offset by several beautiful voices among the singers.]

The gait of our actors, their adjustment, their representative deportment and their manner of moving on the stage are as ungraceful as their faulty habit of pronouncing words or expressing sentiments. Being so unqualified and grossly defective in the first principles of their art, it is not at all to be wondered at that they never make any progressive advances towards the attainment of those exquisite exertions without which there can be neither dignity nor truth in an action. Performers in an opera have this advantage over the comic, that their execution is settled and restrained by the notes, as was the custom in the ancient tragedies; and thus have they marked out for them the path which they are to follow, and therefore they cannot err in regard to the different inflexions or duration of the voice upon the words, because all that is carefully directed by the composer. Notwithstanding these boundaries prescribed, an opportunity is always left to an intelligent singer to throw in a great deal of his own; as in a similar manner choreography or the art of dancing does: for at the same time that it points out to its performers the times, the steps and turnings they are to observe in consonance with the notes of the tune they are to be guided by, there is not room for the least hesitation in asserting that it is the dancer himself who is to give the finishing hand and to heighten his execution with those inborn graces which are the very soul of art.

It is even so with the recitative; for besides the gestures, which entirely depend on the actor, there are certain suspensions of the voice, certain short pauses and a certain insisting on one place more than another that cannot be communicated and are therefore resigned over to his sagacity and discretion.[87] For it is in such minute refinements that chiefly consists the delicacy of expression which impresseth the sense of words not only on the mind, but on the hearts of all who hear them.

---

[87] In a letter to the *Mercure de France*, 21 August 1784, Calzabigi, librettist of the first reform opera *Orfeo ed Euridice,* credited himself with instructing Gluck in just such refinements in the musical composition, suggesting also that these are not entirely matters to be left to the interpreter: 'I read him my *Orfeo*, showing him, by repeating several passages, the nuances that I put into my declamation and that I wanted him to make use of in his composition: the pauses, the slowing down, the speeding up, the sound of the voice now strong, now weaker and in an aside' (tr. in Patricia Howard, *Gluck: an 18th Century Portrait in Letters and Documents,* Oxford 1995, p.56).

Even at this day among the French are remembered excellencies of this nature in the unparalleled acting of their Baron and Le Couvreur[88] that give a heightening to the verses of Corneille and Racine. Their superior strokes of art are ever kept in view and most faithfully imitated in a nation where the theatre now is, as it was formerly in Athens, no inconsiderable object of the public's attention. It would have been an advantage to the Italian stage if our performers had also studied Nicolini's and Tesi's[89] manner of recitative, that is when they kept close to the modesty of nature in expressing her sentiments; but not at all when in order to please too much they indulged in a ranting strain and bordered upon caricature. – The playing to what an actor says, which may be called the dumb show of a scene, is likewise another part of dramatic expression that totally depends upon the actor's judgment; and is as conducive to an enforcing of theatrical illusion as it is necessary that a cause should produce an effect. Everybody knows, without my entering into a detail of proofs, how careless and insignificant in this article are, generally speaking, each Roscius[90] that we see. Their thoughts are bent on everything but on that to which they should solely attend.

Instead of one actor minding what another says to him and marking by the different modifications of gesture and features what impression it has made upon him, he does nothing but smile to the boxes and bow to the company there, with several other such impertinences.[91]

---

[88] Michel Baron (1653-1729), son of an actor and father of actors, was a leading member of Molière's company who played major roles in the works of Corneille and Racine. Adrienne Lecouvreur (1692-1730), likewise a leading actress of the Comédie Française renowned for the naturalness of her declamation, is the heroine of Cilea's well-known opera first presented in 1902 and based on a romanticised version of her life and manner of death by the playwright Eugène Scribe.

[89] The castrato known as Nicolino and the female contralto Vittoria Tesi-Tramontini, both leading 18th century opera singers.

[90] The celebrated Roman actor of the mid 1st century B.C. whose name was once a byword for an actor.

[91] Aaron Hill in the 1730s made similar criticisms: 'The actor who assumes a character wherein he does not seem in earnest to be the person by whose name he calls himself, affronts instead of entertaining the audience ... Have we not a right to the representation we have paid for? And is it possible to be deceived into a mistake of the player for the hero unless he *listens* as well as *speaks*? (quoted in Jean Benedetti, *David Garrick and the Birth of Modern Theatre,* London 2001, p.52: Garrick was renowned as one of the first actors to remain in character throughout a performance, even during a rival's speeches).

By so preposterous a conduct one would think that they had come to a resolution not to impose upon any account or suffer the audience to mistake them for what they really are not: for should one incline to imagine such actors for a time to representatively fill the rank of Achilles, Cyrus etc. on the stage, these dear undeceiving creatures do all in their power to defeat such a pleasing error and declare themselves, as a wag merrily observed, to be no more than the ridiculous signor Petriccino, the silly signor Stoppanino and the zany signor Zolfanello.[56]

This remissness may be assigned perhaps among the principal causes of that extreme disgust, that tyrannizing irksomeness so prevalent at the representation of our operas; against which a remedy has been sought in the perpetual chattering of the company, in visits being made from one box to another, in supping there; and finally in that other remedy which is a thousand times worse than the disease complained of, and that is gaming. All which irregularities will never be removed until such time as what in reality is the first foundation of musical pieces shall no longer be held of no value in the opinion of composers as well as of performers; that is when the recitative, the most essential part of the drama, shall be no longer so disfigured or neglected as at present and when the songs too shall be well acted: then only will operas be heard with delight and force their way to the hearts of an audience.

But in spite of all that connoisseurs may say of acting, the modern performers seem determined to attend to singing only; yet even in that they do not observe the restrictions they should:

E libito fan licito in lor legge,

Knowing no other law but their own will and pleasure.[57] Pistocco, who may be looked upon as the head of the school, the Marini[58] of modern licence-taking, thus

---

[56] These nonsense-names are reminiscent of Benedetto Marcello's satire on the opera, *Il teatro alla moda,* of 1720.
[57] The Italian is a variant of Dante, *Inferno,* Canto 55, v.56: *che libito fé licito in sua legge,* referring to Semiramis, 'who made pleasure licit by her own law.'

rebuked Bernacchi,[95] 'It is very disagreeable to me that although I have taught you to sing, yet you will do the reverse.' It is an old axiom that he who knows not how to bridle his voice can never learn to sing; which indeed our gentry are very careless about. Though to keep the voice sustained in a certain key or to raise it to a certain pitch required by the subject is the great secret of stirring up our affections, yet that they are strangers to, being persuaded on the contrary that all their skill is to consist in straining and splitting the voice and in desultory transitions from one note to another. Their object is not to make choice of what will produce the best effect, but of that which they think the most extraordinary and difficult in the execution.

It is not amiss, to be sure, that young singers apply themselves to become masters of the greatest difficulties in musical execution, because by that means the voice is rendered more obedient to their command on every occasion and grows habituated to perform what was deemed beyond its reach and above its owner's faculties. Moreover it hence follows that the person who can execute the most difficult parts will be certainly qualified to perform what are less so, and through that acquired facility the graces suitable to the subject may be the readier joined by such a proficient.

But to be ever on the tiptoes in straining after difficulties is against the very intention and spirit of the musical art. It is a monstrous inversion of things, making that the end which should only be the means. - It is prescribed by all the rules of taste that the duty of singers is to sing, not to quaver or trill away the sense, but to be intelligible; for by so doing it is no fault of theirs that a musical performance, though it be ever so chaste, so regular and apposite, be dwindled into an unnerved and effeminate composition.

---

[94] Giambattista Marini (or Marino) developed the dominant style in Italian literature of the 17th century, a reaction against Classicism. His delight in complicated word-play and elaborate metaphors, taken further by imitators, came to be known as *Marinism* (or *Secentismo*).

[95] Francesco Pistocchi (1659-1726) was a leading castrato singer of his day who became known also as a teacher of singing. Among his pupils was Antonio Bernacchi (1685-1756), also a celebrated castrato, who on retiring from the stage returned to his native Bologna to open a school of singing: his pupils included the tenor Anton Raaff, the first Idomeneo in Mozart's opera of 1781. For portraits of these two see Angus Heriot, *The Castrati in Opera*, London 1956.

Whether it be that they have never learned, or that they do not like to follow the true precepts of their art, they apply the same graces to every kind of cantilena; and what with their passages, their trillings and besides with their splittings and flights of the voice they overdo, confound and disfigure everything: thus putting, as it were, the same mask on different compositions they so manage matters that all tunes appear to resemble each other; in the same manner as all the ladies in France, by means of the paint and patches, appear to be of the same family.

There is a great liberty allowed by us to a singer, especially in the cantabile songs, which are composed loosely and but with a few notes sufficient to direct the melody, that he may have an opportunity of filling up from himself as he pleases and of throwing in what graces he shall think the best adapted. If one considers the good and the evil which may result from such a practice, the French usage may appear preferable; it never allows their singers such a discretionary power, of which ours indeed make so bad an use. The French bind them down to be the mere performers of others' thoughts, no more. It is true, to hear constantly an exact replication of the same thing must be disagreeable; therefore the most reasonable measure is to leave some occasions for the skill, fancy and feeling of a singer to display themselves: but the mischief of it is that a singer is rarely to be found who, whether through ignorance or through an immoderate lust of pleasing, hath either judgment enough or inclination to be confined to the subject and will not depart from it, forgetful of all decorum and truth. Hundreds of commonplace rhapsodists and of ridiculous heads that thrust in matter foreign from the subject are to be met for one performer in whom knowledge is united with taste, in whom elegance and nature combine and whose fancy is subordinate to his judgment.

To the happy few of that stamp on whom Apollo smiles be it allowed to throw in supplemental touches of their own; because they can best enter into the sense of the composer and are not liable to disagree (as we say) with the bass and movement of the instruments. But for all others not thus qualified let a master be provided that shall write down everything they are to do, leading them by the hand in every variation and in every passage.[96] For this very reason it should not be a matter of so much indifference as it now is to abandon to the singers their conclusive cadenzas, which they most commonly pervert to a quite different meaning and complexion from what was intended by the air: for here the singer is fond of crowding in all the graces, all the difficulties and all the musical tricks he is master of; - ridiculous![97] They should arise naturally from the air and be, as it were, the peroration or epilogue to it.[98]

If our singers were well instructed in their mother tongue, were taught the use of graceful action, were properly initiated in the knowledge of music and, above all, were under due submission to good composers; what then should hinder our hopes of having revived among us that manner of singing which penetrates the soul and of seeing new Sifacis, new Buzzolenis and new Cortonas[99] arise, the memory of whom is not extinct, although their voices be heard no more? If also an expressive melody, accompanied with proper instruments and having good poetry for its basis, were to be executed by singers free from affectation and

---

[96] A study like Tiffany Stern's *Rehearsal from Shakespeare to Sheridan*, Oxford 2000, shows how in the days before professional theatre directors it was poets and playwrights who often took a leading part in instructing and rehearsing actors. In this context it is significant that Gluck regarded his own presence and participation as essential to the success of his later operas and his influence on singers is well documented. Melchior Grimm in his *Correspondence littéraire* complimented Gluck on his training of the tenor Joseph Le Gros, a hitherto indifferent actor, who 'sang the principal role <of Orphée in *Orphée et Euridice*> with such warmth, taste and even soul that it is difficult to recognise him, and his metamorphosis is to be regarded as one of the major miracles wrought by Gluck's magic art' (quoted in Patricia Howard, *Gluck: an 18th Century Portrait in Letters and Documents*, Oxford 1995, p.124). In writing to Du Roullet, his librettist for the French *Alceste*, from Vienna in December 1775, prior to his arrival in Paris for preparations of the work, Gluck says, 'Please tell Mlle. Rosalie <Levasseur, who created the roles of Alceste, Armide and Iphigénie in *Iphigénie en Tauride*> to be sure to learn her role in outline only, because she cannot possibly understand the nuances and the delivery without me; otherwise the correction of bad habits acquired in my absence would be infinitely troublesome to both of us' (*ibid.*, p.155).

[97] The translation omits a comparison Algarotti derived from a treatise on singing of 1723 by Pierfrancesco Tosi, who likens the customary cadenza to a firework display from the terrace of the Castel Sant' Angelo by the Vatican in Rome, culminating in a final outburst (*la girandola*) which sent out 45,000 rockets.

[98] In a new footnote in the 1764 version Algarotti mentions that this opinion, as well as his ideas on the opera overture, were opposed in an essay on the freedom of musicians by D'Alembert. He says that for that reason he would have considered his own views mistaken had they not been supported by 'several outstanding masters of music.' He quotes from the essay again at the beginning of chapter 5: see footnote 111.

[99] Leading singers of the late 17th and early 18th centuries, the castrati known as Siface and Cortona (for portraits see Angus Heriot, *op. cit.*) and the tenor Giovanni Buzzoleni.

animated by gestures both fitting and noble, then music would be invested with the arbitrary power of exciting or calming our passions; and then should we see renewed in our times similar effects to those which that enrapturing art had caused among the ancients, and for this apparent reason of her enjoying now the auxiliary concomitants. But it would be folly in us to hope for obtaining by one single article what requires the concurrence of many.[100]

It is not to be doubted that whenever music shall be restored to her pristine dignity operas will be honoured with the attention of the public and be heard with the greatest delight from the beginning to the end, because then a grateful silence will be imposed on all spectators; whereas quite the contrary is now observable in our theatres; on entering one of which so great a confusion and uproar is heard as to resemble the bellowing of a wood in a storm, or the roaring of the sea to a tempestuous wind.[101] Even the most attentive of our now opera-frequenters can be silent only to hear some air of Bravura; but they are all desire at the dances, which can never begin too soon for their impatience nor last too long for their enjoying them; so that it may now be asserted of the dances that they have taken possession

---

[100] [Author's note:] 'We are to consider that the music with the ancients was of a larger extent than what we call music nowadays, for poetry and dancing or [comely motion] were then accounted parts of music, when music arrived to some perfection - what we now call music is but what they called harmonic, which was but one part of their music (consisting of words, verse, voice, tune, instrument and acting); and we are not to expect the same effect of one piece as of the whole.' – *Strange effects reported of music in former times examined by Dr, Wallis – Philosophical Transactions* abridged by John Lowthorp, Vol. I, pp.618-619. [John Wallis (1616-1703) was a cleric and Oxford mathematician under both the Commonwealth and Restoration.]

[101] [Author's note:]
Garganum mugire putes nemus aut mare Tuscum:
Tanto cum strepitu ludi spectantur et artes.
[Horace, Epistles II, 1, vv.20f.: 'you would think it was the Garganian grove or the Tuscan sea roaring, such a clamour they make when viewing the games and other arts.' Algarotti used this quotation as an epigraph for his essay in its original 1755 version, no doubt intending to allude to the behaviour of contemporary opera audiences. The title page then and in the later editions carried a quotation from Ovid, Metamorphoses I, v.398: *sed quid temptare nocebit?* Deucalion and Pyrrha, the only survivors of the primeval great flood, have been instructed by the gods to throw stones behind them that will be transformed into people to restock the earth. Deucalion is sceptical, but complies: 'what harm will it be to make the attempt?' Algarotti may imply an ironical analogy to his attempt in the essay to throw out suggestions for reanimating the world of opera, submerged as it is under the weight of moribund convention.]

of the spectators' hearts as well as of their eyes.[102] It seems indeed as if our theatre had been intended rather for an academy of dancing than the representation of an opera, and one would be induced to think that the Italians have adopted the Frenchman's advice who said, not unpleasantly, that in order to make the theatre flourish, the dances should be lengthened and the women's petticoats made shorter.[103]

---

[102] [Author's note:]
        Verum equitis quoque iam migravit ab aure voluptas
        Omnis ad incertos oculos et gaudia vana.
[*ibid.*, vv.187f.: now it is no longer the ears of the knights that experience every kind of pleasure, but rather it is their wandering eyes that take in empty delights.]

[103] There is a certain irony in this remark considering that the censorship in pre-unification Italy was often exercised by questions of possible "obscenities" in opera performances, which John Rosselli interprets as 'ballet dancers showing too much leg.' He records that 'the Imperial Royal Provincial Delegation at Padua was only one of several authorities to express indignation on this score (pointing to the number of university students in the audience): at such times the impresario might be ordered to have the dancers' skirts lengthened'! (*The Opera Industry in Italy from Cimarosa to Verdi: the Role of the Impresario,* Cambridge 1984, p.94).

CHAPTER IV

OF THE DANCES

What is the essence and nature of Dancing, which people run so passionately after? It never was a constituent part of the drama, is always foreign from the business and very often repugnant to it. As soon as an act is over several dancers sally forth on the stage who have no matter of affinity with the plan of the piece. For if the scene of action be in Rome, the dance is often made to be in Cusco[104] or Peking, and if the opera be serious, the dance to be sure is comic. Nothing can be imagined so devoid of a methodical proceeding, of explanatory connection, or that is carried on with such irregular bounds from one appearance to another, or is so much a stranger to (if it is not profaning the word on such an occasion) the law of continuity, an inviolable law of nature, and which it is the duty of all the imitative arts never to transgress.

But no more on that head, because in the present licentiousness of taste it might be rebuked as the sophistry of hypercriticism: therefore let us to the point. The dancing which delights some people so much is in itself (as now used by us) nothing better than irrational caprioling from the beginning to the very end, an illiberal skipping about, which ought never to be applauded by persons of a polite education, being as it were a perpetual monotony of a very few steps and as few figures. The wonted custom now is that after the preluding flourish of a very disagreeable tune a couple of young men are detached on the stage from the dancing band, all in readiness behind the scenes: and it is the hackneyed practice that one of them robs the other of a nosegay, some flowers, etc., or plays him a trick of this sort; they grow angry with each other, but soon become reconciled, although they stop not for a moment to settle the matter: then one invites the other to dance and to it they go like mad folks, without the least moderation. After the

---

[104] Or Cuzco, ancient capital of the Inca empire in Peru, a typically exotic location.

first two have done their task, two of larger size come on, who are succeeded by the two chief dancers; they likewise perform a dance of the same complexion; and it is epilogued by the latter part of the tune, which is to the full as bad as its beginning. Whoever knows one dance knows them all; for though dancers may change their dresses, the characters introduced are seldom varied.

Whoever, as far as relates to the art of dancing, would let his judgment be warped by what he sees in vogue with Italians and would not raise his thoughts higher must be induced to consider as fabulous relations many things that are nevertheless founded upon truth: those accounts, for example, which are to be read in authors of the very tragic effects that had been caused in Athens by the dance of the Eumenides,[105] as well as of the powerful energy transfused into others by the amazing skill and execution of Pylades and Batillus; one of whom could excite pity or terror by dancing, the other could provoke jollity and laughter. These divided Rome into two parties in the reign of Augustus.[106]

It happens but very rarely that in our Italian dancers strength of body is united with a gracefulness of figure; or a delicate display of the arms with a dextrous activity in the feet; or that a certain ease and gentle sway appear in their movements; without which concomitants dancing is a fatigue not only to the performers, but even to the spectators. Yet these are nothing more than the rudiments of the art, or, to speak with more propriety, the requisite materials; but the final accomplishing of and tasteful form suitable to the subject is another thing, and requires great delicacy of judgment in the contrivance.

The art of dancing ought to be imitative of nature and of the affections of the mind by the body's moving to musical numbers. It is her office to speak continually and point to the eyes. A dance, moreover, should have its exposition,

---

[105] The ancient *Life of Aeschylus* records that the appearance of the Eumenides, or Furies, in the third part of his Oresteian trilogy was so frightening at the first performance at Athens in 458 B.C. that women in the audience miscarried.

[106] Pylades and Bathyllus were highly acclaimed exponents, serious and comic respectively, of the art of the *pantomimus*, or mimic dancer, towards the end of the 1st century B.C. in Rome who enjoyed the patronage and protection of Augustus Caesar. He opened an imperial theatre for their performances – an example of the policy of providing 'bread and circuses' to win popular favour.

its intricacy and dénouement; it ought to be the quintessential abridgement of an action. A brilliant example of what we have here advanced is the dance of *The Gamester,* composed on an admirable air of Jommelli, in which are wonderfully expressed all the incidents in the charming intermezzo called by the same name.[107]

It is but just, however, to own that in the comic, or rather perhaps the grotesque style, we have had dances composed among us worthy of applause; and dancers of whom it might be said that they were eloquent both in hands and feet, and whose execution was not perhaps inferior to that of Batillus.

But for composing and performing both serious and heroic dances, not only we Italians, but all the other nations of Europe must strike to the French. For what people in the modern world both applied themselves so studiously as they have to excel in the art of dancing, for which indeed they seem to be fitted by nature, as Italians are for music? Choreography, or the art of dancing, took its rise among them about the end of the fifteenth century, and in these latter times they have produced the ballet of a La Rose, Ariane, Pygmalion[108] and many others that approach very near to the excellence of Pylades and of the most celebrated ancient pantomimes.

The French are the acknowledged masters in this school of the imitative arts, nor ought any other nation to be ashamed to take lessons from them in this article of polite accomplishment. We Italians in particular may without ceremony receive

---

[107] The comic intermezzo *Bacocco e Serpilla* of 1715 by Giuseppe Maria Orlandini was one of the most frequently performed musical dramatic works of the whole 18th century. As *The Gamester* it was played in London in 1737 and as *Il giocatore* at the Comédie Italienne in Paris in 1752. In its various incarnations it was sometimes supplemented with additional music by other composers, such as the piece by Jommelli mentioned here.

[108] *Ariane* may refer to an *entrée* in the ballet, *Les amours des dieux,* of 1727 by Jean-Joseph Mouret; there was an earlier work of the same name by Robert Cambert, whose *Pomone* of 1671 was the first French opera. To Mouret also is attributed the music of a ballet on the story of Pygmalion of 1734, an historically important piece in that in it the famous Marie Sallé appeared for the first time bare-headed and wearing a simple muslin dress instead of the customary elaborate costume. The reference may be to *Pigmalion,* an *acte de ballet* by Rameau of 1748, one of his most popular and frequently performed works. It is not clear to what the ballet of *La Rose* refers.

from the French wherewith to render our opera exhibition less imperfect, since to us the French are indebted for the very institution of theirs.[109]

---

[109] The immediate precursor to Gluck's *Orfeo ed Euridice* was his ballet *Don Juan*, presented at Vienna in October 1751. The scenario and choreography by the imperial ballet-master Gasparo Angiolini were inspired by the work of Jean-Georges Noverre, the first to try to make of ballet a choreographic drama. The latter was responsible for the danced scenes in some of Rameau's operas and is known to have admired the naturalistic acting of David Garrick: see Patricia Howard, *C. W. von Gluck, Orfeo* (Cambridge Opera Handbooks), Cambridge 1981, p.13. Through Angiolini and Guadagni, the first Orfeo, Garrick can be said to have had some influence on reform opera, as Daniel Heartz shows: cf. his *From Garrick to Gluck: the Reform of Theatre and Opera in the Mid-18th Century*, Proceedings of the Royal Musical Assocation, London, Vol. XCIV (1967), pp.111-127, esp. pp.124ff.

CHAPTER V

ON SCENERY, DRESS, ETC.

To the many improprieties with which the dances now abound may be added those observable in the ornaments and dresses of the dancers: their dresses, as well as those of the singers, ought to approach as near as possible to the manners of the times and nations which are represented; I say as near as possible because the stage must be allowed occasionally some liberties; and in this article, more than in any other, ought it to avoid the imputation of stiffness and pedantry. If, on the one hand, it is not expected that our artists plan out, hit exactly and trim up a toga or chlamys in so accurate a manner as they are described by the learned Ferrario;[110] yet, on the other, they never should be permitted to put pipes into the mouths and Dutch breeches on the posteriors of Aeneas' Trojan companions.[111] But in order that dresses should be appropriated according to the custom of a country and be well fancied at the same time, the assistance of a Julio Romano and a Tribolo[112] would be wanted, because in that article they have given proof of

---

[110] Possibly Defendente Ferrari, an Italian artist of the first half of the 16th century artist who drew inspiration from German literature and Flemish painting.

[111] [Author's note 1764:] *Un de nos plus grands artistes, qui ne sera pas soupçonné d'ignorer la belle nature par ceux qui ont vu ses ouvrages, a renoncé aux spectacles que nos appellons sérieux et qu'il n'appelle pas du même nom; la manière ridicule, dont les Dieux et les Héros y sont vêtus, dont ils y agissent, dont ils y parlent, dérange toutes les idées qu'il s'en est faites; il n'y retrouve point ces Dieux et ces Héros, auxquels son ciseau sait donner tant de noblesse et tant d'âme, et il est réduit à chercher son délassement dans les spectacles de farce, dont les tableaux burlesques sans prétension, ne laissent dans sa tête aucune trace nuisible.* M. D'Alembert, *de la Liberté de la Musique,* Art. XIV dans une note. ['One of our greatest artists, who would not be suspected of ignoring the beauties of nature by those who have seen his works, has given up the spectacles that we call serious, but which he does not call by the same name. The ridiculous manner in which gods and heroes are costumed in such spectacles, the way they behave and talk, upset every idea he has of them. He cannot find there at all the gods and heroes to whom by his chisel he knows how to give such nobility and such qualities of soul, and he is reduced to finding his entertainment in comic shows, whose humour and unpretentious depictions leave in his head no trace of annoyance.' The essay of D'Alembert *On the Freedom of Music* appears in the fourth volume of his *Mélanges de literature, d'histoire et de philsophie*, published at Amsterdam in 1759.]

[112] Giulio Romano (c.1499-1546), painter and architect, was one of Raphael's foremost pupils; Niccolò Pericoli, known as Il Tribolo (1500-1558), was a Florentine sculptor.

their skill, or at least it would be necessary that the persons who superintend the wardrobe-department were blessed with a kindred genius to those eminent artists.

It would have been still more necessary for our modern painters to copy after a San Gallo and a Peruzzi,[113] because we consequently should not see in our theatres the temple of Jupiter or Mars bear a resemblance to the church of Jesus, nor would the architecture of a piazza in Carthage have a Gothic complexion, for in all scene-painting the costume and propriety must be united. The scenery is the first object in an opera that powerfully attracts the eye, that determines the place of action and co-operates chiefly to the illusive enchantment, that makes the spectator imagine himself to be transported either to Egypt, to Greece, to Troy, to Mexico, to the Elysian Fields or even up to Olympus.

Who does not now perceive of what importance it is that the painter's imagination should be regulated by learning and guided by a correct judgment? To this will greatly contribute the perusal of authors and conversation of learned men well skilled in the customs of antiquity. But the artist should have recourse to no person preferably to the poet, the author of the opera, who, we are to suppose, has preconceived in his mind every article and to have omitted nothing that can help to embellish or make the action he has chosen to exhibit appear probable.

Although the painters of the fifteenth century are without doubt the most excellent, yet the art of scene-painting received considerable improvements in the last age, and the obvious reason is that many theatres then erected gave occasion to that species of painting to become more common; whence it necessarily followed that a great number of ingenious persons, applying themselves to it, have brought it nearer to perfection. The devised contrivances of Girolamo Genga (extolled so much by Serlio[114]) to make, in the theatre of Urbino, trees etc. of the

---

[113] Antonio da Sangallo (1455-1534), who came from a Florentine family of architects, designed the *Palazzo Farnese* in Rome for Pope Paul III. Baldassare Peruzzi (1481-1536), a contemporary of Raphael from Siena, was one of the first to attempt architectural illusion in painting, the so-called *quadratura*.

[114] Girolamo Genga (1479-1551), painter and sculptor of Urbino, assistant to Perugino whose painting was much influenced by Raphael, was also a skilled musician. Sebastiano Serlio (1475-1554) introduced Roman architectural principles into France. Jean-Philippe Navarre (*op. cit.*, p.127) points out that Algarotti refers here to a passage on Genga in the second book of Serlio's

finest silk would nowadays be classed among the childish baubles that adorn the manger in the shows of Christ's nativity. It is further my opinion that Serlio, from whose treatise upon scenery there may nevertheless some good hints be taken, did not sufficiently consider how, without the assistance of relievos in wood, we might conquer all the difficulties of perspective, and how, in very confined situations, we could represent the appearance of an extensive space; for to such a pitch the science of deceiving the eye has been improved in our time. The introduction especially of accidental points, or rather the invention of viewing scenes by the angle, produces the finest effects imaginable, but that requires the nicest judgment to bring properly into practice. *Ferdinando Bibiena*[115] was the inventor of those scenes which, by the novelty of the manner, drew the eyes of all the curious upon him. They soon began to look upon, as unpleasing objects for a stage, those streets and narrow passages, those galleries that were always made to tend to its centre, there at once to limit the spectator's imagination and sight.

He had studied the principles of his art in Vignola[116] under good masters: moreover, being endowed with a picturesque and animating fancy, he came to a resolution of giving a meaning to his scenes, after the same manner as had been done before him, by the painters of the fifteenth century, to the figures of Bellini, Perrugi and Mantegna.[117]

Ferdinando Bibiena was the Paul Veronese of the theatre; and like him he enjoyed the glory of raising his art to the summit, so far as relates to the magnificent and to a certain degree of the marvellous. He had the luck too, like Veronese, of not establishing it by the pupils reared up under him. They employed

---

writings on architecture dealing with landscape, a passage near the end of the third chapter which has a print showing several buildings set in a wood with a central avenue. Apart from the trees Serlio also mentions on silks of different colours flowers, a water-course decorated with frogs, snakes and tortoises, etc.

[115] Ferdinando Galli da Bibiena (1657-1743), the most renowned of a family of artists, was celebrated throughout Europe for his architectural views and theatrical designs, as well for his magnificent designs for public and court festivities. He wrote several treatises on architecture and in stage design was particularly noted for his ability to create an illusion of depth in stage sets.

[116] A town near Bologna. Giovanni da Vignola (d.1573) was a precursor of Baroque architecture.

all their pains in imitating the easiest part of his manner, which was the whimsical, forgetting the fundamentals of the art by which means only things are rendered probable: therefore in professing to follow they went quite astray from their master.

The most new-fangled whims, the most out-of-the-way conceits[118] that could be imagined were the objects they delighted to represent; and, not to mention a certain arbitrary perspective of their own creation, they bestowed the name of cabinet on what ought to be called a large saloon or a hall, and the name of prison on what might serve for a portico, or rather for a piazza.

Vitruvius related the following anecdote of a painter employed at Tralles to execute a scene. He introduced therein some things that, without sinning against verisimilitude, could have no place there. The citizens, however, were about honouring his performance with their approbation, it being in some parts finished in a very masterly manner. But all on a sudden one Licinius, a mathematician, by thus accosting them, opened their eyes, 'Do ye not perceive, my fellow citizens, that if ye should praise in pictures what can neither stand the scrutiny of the judicious or be warranted by taste, your city will run a great risk of being ranked among those that are not remarkable for a keenness of understanding?'[119]

What would that mathematician say were he now alive on hearing so much applause lavished by us on those labyrinths of architecture, those crowded buildings with which our scenes are surcharged, and from which all semblance of truth is excluded; or those unwieldy fabrics that appear neither to stand upright, nor to have a settled foundation; and where the columns, having their architraves topsy-turvey, and jumbled with the roof, lose themselves in a sea of clouding rags,

---

[117] [Author's note:] The writer of this essay hath in his possession a large volume of designs of the same artist, which are a more evincing proof of his superior merit than those engravings that are carried about in his name and executed by Buffagnoti and Abbati.

[118] *Ghiribizzi* in the Italian. The translator omits a list of near-synonyms offered by Algarotti - *trabiccoli, centinamenti, tritumi, trafori* - a rhetorical device of literary Italian that he evidently did not think would reproduce well in English.

[119] Book VII, ch. 5. Vitruvius goes on to say that on the advice of Licinius, or Licymnius, the painter in question altered his design to make it more realistic and so won greater approval. The quotation in the next footnote follows this passage in Vitruvius' text.

suspended in mid-air. The like blundering is visible in the volutes, being executed in so defective and lame a manner. But even among us there rises up now and then a Licinius.[120] For something similar to what had happened to the above mentioned painter was the case of father Pozzi[121], one of the masters in the modern school. In his picture of a cupola he made the columns to lean upon little props, which was ridiculed by several architects, declaring that for any consideration they would not have done the like in a real structure. Nevertheless they were made to alter their opinion, as he himself relates, by a friend of his, who offered to bind himself to pay all expenses of an experiment to be made if, in striking away such props, the columns should fall. However that is but a poor excuse, as if architecture were not to be painted according to rule, and as if what offends in a reality would not offend the imagination in a picture.

To keep their conceptions within the boundaries of prudence, it will be expedient for painting artists never to be tired of studying those venerable pieces of ancient architecture that are yet standing. India can furnish them also with several noble examples, as can likewise Greece. To her we are indebted for the revival of correct architecture. Even Egypt, the first mistress of all polite institutions, can supply many useful hints. And in effect what can be more superb and awful, not to mention the pyramids, than the remains of Memnon's palace, that tower along the banks of the river Nile, or of that ancient city Thebes with an hundred gates; all which the public can now enjoy by the means of Norden's accurate performance.[122] They are admirable not only in their forms, but in the chaste ornaments which they receive from the colossal parts and the sphinxes that accompany them, because therein most conspicuously appears the Tuscan

---

[120] [Author's note:] *Utinam Dii immortales fecissent, ut Licinius revivisceret et corrigeret hanc amentiam*: Would to the immortal Gods that Licinius were to rise up again to correct this madness.
[121] Andrea Pozzo (1642-1709), fresco painter and architect, whose work displayed typically Baroque effects of perspective and illusion.
[122] [Author's note:] See his *Travels into Egypt*. [Frederick Ludvig Norden (1708-1742) was a Danish naval officer whose *Travels in Egypt and Nubia* were published in two volumes at Copenhagen in 1755.]

manner;[123] and if they were sometimes properly introduced on the stage, they would produce amazing effects.

China also, that ancient nursery of the arts, peopled, as some will have it, by a colony from Egypt, may also furnish very beautiful scenes. But, as I have above objected against the exhibition of any capricious and fantastical combinations, which, to the disgrace of our national taste, have got too great a footing among us and have supplanted the learnedly grotesque compositions of Giovanni da Udine[124] and of other contemporary masters with him, I do not mean here that our painters should imitate either pagodas or towers of porcelain, unless the subject of the opera be Chinese.[125]

The objects I purpose to recommend to the imitation of our artists, from which pleasing ideas will arise and delightful scenes may be drawn, are the gardens of that most ingenious nation; for the gardeners there are so many painters who do not lay out their ground with the same regularity which architects observe in building houses; no, they take nature for their guide and employ all their efforts to imitate her noble disregard of symmetric order and her fondness of variety.

Their favourite practice is to make a choice of those objects which in their several kinds are most entertaining to the eye. Then they arrange them in such a manner as that the one may be a contrast to the other and that from the whole may result something new and uncommon. In their little woods there is painted a lively intermixture of those trees which are of a different appearance, condition, colour and nature. What a variety of situations do they contrive to exhibit in one place! Here we are alarmed on viewing rocks cut in so artificial a manner as to appear pendulous in air, or cascades of water bursting from caverns and grottoes, where they know how to make the light play in various ways. In another part we are charmed with the sight of flowery parterres, limpid canals, lovely islands crowned with pretty edifices, whose reflection is seen in the water. Thus from the most

---

[123] The Italian original also has 'Herculean and Michelangelesque' as alternatives to 'Tuscan.'
[124] Fresco-painter (1487-1546) epitomising the "grotesque" style that fancifully mixes various forms.
[125] As for example Gluck's *Le cinesi* of 1754 with libretto by Metastasio.

horrid prospects they waft us in a moment to the most enchanting, and from the marvellous the delightful is never separate; to produce which effect in a garden costs them as much application and study as an author is subject to in composing the fable of a poem.

The English have derived their present taste in gardening from the Chinese, by which means it is that their Kent and Chambers have so far surpassed Le Nôtre, who before their time was esteemed to be the unrivalled master of the art of laying out gardens.[126] French regularity is now banished from all villas in England. The most delightful situations there have the complexion of nature. Cultivated ground is intermixed with parts neglected, and a seeming irregularity is the effect of consummate art.[127]

---

[126] William Kent (1685-1748) and William Chambers (1723-1796) were pioneers of the English style of landscape gardening following natural contours that is associated especially with Lancelot "Capability" Brown (1715-1783), a pupil of Kent at Stowe: his name is added by Algarotti to those of Kent and Chambers in the 1764 edition of the essay. The style was an early Romantic reaction against the formality of such gardens as those at the palace of Versailles, designed by André Le Nôtre (1613-1700). In view of what Algarotti says here it is interesting to note that Chambers, whose pagoda at Kew is well known and who also designed the present Somerset House, had travelled in China and published in 1757 his *Designs of Chinese Buildings*.

[127] [Author's note:]
On a bad taste in gardens
        His gardens next our admiration call;
        On every side you look behold the wall.
        No pleasing intricacies intervene,
        No artful wildness to perplex the scene:
        Grove nods at grove, each alley has a brother,
        And half the platform just reflects the other.

On a good taste in gardens
        Consult the genius of the place in all,
        That tells the waters or to rise or fall,
        Or helps the ambitious hill the heavens to scale,
        Or scoops in circling theatres the vale;
        Calls in the country, catches open glades,
        Joins willing woods and varies shades from shades;
        Now breaks, or now directs the intending lines,
        Paints as you plant, and as you work designs.
        Pope, *Epistle to the Earl of Burlington* [vv.113-118 and 57-64.

Pope's own summary of his poem suggests that good taste consists in following Nature 'instanced in architecture and gardening, where all must be adapted to the genius and use of the place, and the beauties not forced into it, but resulting from it.' Without this true foundation 'the best examples and rules will but be perverted into something burdensome or ridiculous.' The first grand error of the false taste of magnificence 'is to imagine that greatness consists in the size and dimension,

But to return nearer home, what is the reason our painters do not study those objects that are under their eyes? Besides the ancient edifices still subsisting in Italy the elegant fabrics erected in modern times might often be introduced on the scenes without incurring the charge of impropriety. And likewise why do they not study those plans of architecture that adorn many of Paolo's pictures, by which he may be said to have rendered the events of history theatrical? Why also do they not study the landscapes of Poussin, of Titian, Marchetto Ricci and Claudio,[128] who all possessed the secret of observing and collecting from nature her most valuable and attractive appearances? Finally I would advise those painters unendowed with imaginative powers to betake themselves to copying the pieces of the before-mentioned masters; and in so doing they would imitate that worthy churchman who, rather than pester an audience with his own nonsensical sermons, got by heart and repeated to them those of Segneri.[129]

Another most important article, not so much attended to as it should, is in the not leaving convenient openings in the scenes, particularly of architecture, that the actors may come on and go off the stage in such a manner as that their figures may appear to an observer's eye to be in a just proportion with the columns. We often see them obliged to advance from the bottom of the stage, because it is there that the only entrance is contrived for them, which makes their persons shew very incongruous and offensive to a discerning spectator. The apparent magnitude of

---

instead of the proportion and harmony of the whole, and the second, either in joining together parts incoherent, or too minutely resembling, or in the repetition of the same too frequently.' These precepts of Pope, an acquaintance of Algarotti, writing in 1731, are an instance of the same reaction against the artificiality of the Baroque and towards a greater naturalism in the arts that informs Algarotti's reflections on opera. The poem was occasioned by the publication of a volume by Lord Burlington of designs of Palladio. Burlington's Palladian mansion of Chiswick House had gardens laid out with help from Kent, while Pope's own garden at Twickenham was another early example of the naturalistic English style. For the complete epistle see *The Poems of Alexander Pope*, ed. John Butt, London 1963, pp.586-595].

[128] Of the artists mentioned here Paolo is Veronese and Claudio Claude Lorrain. Marchetto or Marco Ricci (1676-1729) was a Venetian landscape painter. A series of 24 prints of views of Venice and the surrounding countryside taken from works of Ricci by the later artist Fossati was dedicated to Algarotti in 1743. Paintings by Ricci can be seen at Castle Howard.

[129] Paolo Segneri the Elder (1624-1694), a Jesuit missionary renowed as one of the foremost Italian preachers and orators of his day. His much reprinted *Quaresimale* won the admiration of the future Pope Innocent XII, while an English translation by "Father Humphrey" of his *Panegyrici sacri* appeared in 1877.

an object depends on a judicious comparison made of the exhibited figure with its distance from us. So a figure, being supposed of such a magnitude, the farther it is distant from us the greater the object will be esteemed. And hence may be assigned the reason why the performers, presenting themselves from the bottom of the stage, appear like so many towering giants by the artificial magic of the scene, through the illusive power of perspective, inducing us to fancy them at a prodigious distance. Yet these imaginary giants dwindle by degrees as they come forward and are dwarfed down to their native size as they approach nearer to us.

The same remark holds good in regard to attendants, guards etc., who should never be made to enter at that part of the stage where the capitals of the columns rise no higher than their shoulders, or perhaps their sword-belts, which defeats all deception intended by the scenery. Let this be a general caution:- it requires the greatest circumspection in a director where it is necessary to blend falsehood with truth; for if the one give the lie to the other a discovery ensues, and the whole is rejected as an intended imposition.

There yet remains an article to be mentioned and of equal importance with the foregoing, though not sufficiently considered, and that erroneously, to wit, the illumination of the scenes. What wonderful things might not be produced by the light, when not dispensed in what equal manner and by degrees as is now the custom. Were it to be played off with a masterly artifice, distributing it in a strong mass on some parts of the stage and by depriving others, as it were, at the same time, it is hardly credible what effects might be produced thereby: for instance, a *chiaro obscuro* for strength and vivacity not inferior to that so much admired in the prints of Rembrandt.

And pray, why might not a representation of the pleasing mixtures of light and shade in the pictures of Giorgione or of Titian be found practicable on the stage? Nay, the more so when we call to mind those little portable theatres, carried about under the names of mathematical optic-views, that represent seaports, fleets engaged etc. Therein the light is admitted through an oiled paper that deadens the rays which might prove too striking, and by that means is so attempered that its various rays greatly consociate and are reflected with the greatest harmony.

I also remember to have seen (on the occasion of shewing one of the holy sepulchres, according to a practice at Bologna) some very coarse pictures upon the walls of the church and some contemptible statues that seemed no better than as if made of bundles of coarse paper, which nevertheless, by receiving the light through some oiled papers from lanterns, appeared, although near our eyes, to be finished to the life and of the purest marble.

Whenever a theatre shall be illuminated in the manner it ought, then will manifestly triumph the great advantage our dramatic representations by night have over those of the ancients, which were by day; and then no doubt but the scenery, displayed in such a theatre, being executed by the most eminent painters, remarkable too for their propriety and elegance, will not only please above, but even supersede all those capricious stage exhibitions that have shamefully been hitherto so much in vogue and are even now so much extolled by certain would-be connoisseurs, who examine nothing yet decide upon everything.

Then such a revolution will happen in the Italian as once happened in the French theatre when after the long reign of Spanish absurdities, which were a disgrace to Thalia, her favourite Molière's judicious and natural comic pieces appeared. Rapid was the success they obtained through that resistless power which truth has upon the minds of mankind when once they are made acquainted with her. At that glorious epoch did the learned Menagius[130] exultingly cry out, 'at last the time is come to knock down those idols before whose unhallowed shrines the misled natives of France have so long burnt incense.'

---

[130] I.e. Gilles Ménage, known also in Latin as Aegidius Menagius (1613-1692), French scholar who frequented Mme. de Rambouillet's circle of *précieuses* and was known for his own "mercuriales," Wednesday literary meetings which he sponsored for over thirty years.

CHAPTER VI

ON THE STRUCTURE OF THEATRES

Thus far we have treated of all the constituent parts of an opera that want to be corrected and stand greatly in need of a thorough reformation. The desire of pleasing too much was the principal cause of each straying beyond its due bounds, by which transgressions they have spoilt a composition whose beauty should result from all the parts being properly adjusted together and amicably co-operating with each other.

From the same source too another fault has sprung, and that is when in these latter times an opportunity of building a new theatre presented itself, architecture, seized by the same contagious distemper, instead of considering the use and intent for which the structure was proposed, thought of nothing but giving a loose to ornamental achievings and all the expensive pomp of her art; which indeed rendered such edifices beautiful to the eyes of common beholders, but to the judicious they appeared culpable, because deviating from their intent.

As many debates upon this head set the curious about enquiring what were the fittest materials to build a theatre with, as well as about the dimensions and form it ought to have and the dispositions of the boxes, and how they should be decorated, it will not be departing from our subject to examine those articles a little. For since as far as in our power lay the requisite form of an opera has been delineated, it is not improper now to determine the most commodious form that can be given to the fabric in which it is to be exhibited for the joint entertainment of our sight and hearing.

In regard to the first article, the materials, we cannot but very much approve the practice of those who in building theatres contrive that the galleries and the stairs be of brick or stone: for besides the perpetuity such materials give to a building, they are its best insurance against fire, to which they are more liable than any other kind of structure.[131] Why then, whether for the sake of the fabric's perpetuity, or through a mistaken notion of magnificence, have not some artists taken it into their heads to make the boxes and the interior parts looking towards the stage of stone? - Because such a proceeding would militate against the chief end an architect should propose to himself in erecting a theatre, to wit that its sonority should be such as that the voices of the singers may be heard as distinct as possible and rendered at the same time both melodious and pleasing to the ears of an audience.

Daily experience teacheth us that in a box whose walls are naked the singer's voice is reverberated in a particular matter; it sounds crude and harsh and by no means flattering to the ear. The accents are quite lost if the box be hung with tapestry; whereas they are reflected full, sonorous and agreeable to the ear when the boxes are only boarded; which is an obvious proof, and confirmed by experience, that the best lining for the interior part of a theatre is wood, and preferably that species of which musical instruments are made, on account of its being more apt than any other when struck by sound to be agitated by the kind of vibrations that are the most analogous with the organ of hearing.

The ancients, it is true, had vases made of bronze fixed in certain places of their theatres, in order to increase the sound of the actor's voice; but such edifices, among them, were made of solid materials, viz. stone, cement or marble, which are by no means resounding: while, on the contrary, such resources were unnecessary in those made of wood, whose gift it is, as Vitruvius asserts, to reflect sounds.[132] And thus this great master among the ancients comes now, as it were,

---

[131] [Author's note:] In Italy [though not only there, one might add].

[132] [Author's note:] *Itaque ex hac indagationibus mathematicis rationibus fiunt vasa arca, pro ratione magnitudini theatri. – Dicet aliquis forte multa theatra Roma quotannis facta esse, neque ullam rationem earum rerum in his fuisse; sed errat in eo, quod omnia publica lignea theatra tabulationibus habet complures, quas necesse est sonare. – Cum autem ex solidis rebus theatra constituunt, id est, ex structura caementorum, lapide, marmore, quae sonare non possunt, tunc ex his hac ratione sunt explicanda.* Vitruvius, Book 5, ch. 5. ['And so in accordance with these investigations on mathematical principles bronze vessels are made in proportion to the size of the theatre. ... Somebody will perhaps say that many theatres have been built each year in Rome and that in them no attention has been paid to these principles, but he would be in error, seeing that all the public theatres made of wood have a great deal of boarding, which must be resonant. ... But

by the rebound to teach us moderns what are the proper materials for constructing a theatre. Be it however remembered that wood so employed ought to be properly seasoned and to be made throughout equally smooth and even; by which expedient the vibrations will not come riding, as one may say, one upon the other; and that wood will reverberate the sonorous rays in the most regular manner whose every fibre is vibrated alike.

Many persons think that the vastness of a theatre contributes much to its beauty. It is certain that large edifices have wherewithal to surprise and please the human mind, but it is necessary that in this article, as well as in every other, certain regulations and boundaries should be observed.

The extent of a place, Vitriuvius declares, should always be in proportion to the multitude of the inhabitants, so that on the one hand the space allotted should not be too narrow for conveniency and use, and on the other, through the fewness of the people, the forum should not appear solitary and unfrequented.[133] Now without insisting upon the absurdity of a large theatre being built for a small district, let us consider that the measure of the length of the parterre or pit and size of a theatre is the performers' reach of voice and none other. For it would be equally ridiculous in any person to have a theatre built so large as that people could not hear in it, as in an engineer to make the works of a fortress in such a manner as that they could not be defended; which will always be the case when the line of defence, or the length of the curtain that ought to be the module for all the parts of a fortification, are not made in a due reference to the reach of the musketry.

That the ancients had theatres much larger than ours is not to be doubted; wherefore, besides the vases of bronze which they made use of to strengthen the voice, the mouth of the masks which the actors wore were contrived so as to spread themselves outwards like a speaking trumpet: by such devices the natural

---

when theatres are made of solid materials, such as masonry, stone or marble, which cannot be resonant, the foregoing principles must be applied.']

[133] [Author's note:] *Magnitudines autem ad copias hominum oportet fieri, ne parvum spatium sit ad usum, aut ne propter inopiam populi vastum forum videatur.* Book 5, ch. 1.

power of the voice was greatly increased. But we, being deprived of such assistance, must confine ourselves to narrower bounds, since who would be desirous of hearing the voice raised like to that of a crier? In other words, who would be desirous of truth disfigured by a misrepresentation of nature?

As most people are captivated with what appears grand and magnificent, some were induced to resolve on having a theatre built of an excessive extent, and out of all reason, where, however, they should hear commodiously; which to effect they made the stage whereon the actors perform to be advanced into the parterre several feet; by that expedient the actors were brought forward into the middle of the audience and there was no danger then of their not being heard. But such a contrivance can only please those who are very easily to be satisfied. For who that reflects does not see that such a proceeding is subversive of all good order and prudent regulation?

The actors, instead of being so brought forwards, ought to be thrown back at a certain distance from the spectator's eye and stand within the scenery of the stage, in order to make a part of that pleasing illusion for which all dramatic exhibitions are calculated. But by such preposterous inversion of things the very intent of theatric representation is destroyed, and the proposed effect defeated, by thus detaching actors from the precincts of the decoration and dragging them forth from the scenes into the midst of the parterre; which cannot be done by them without shewing their sides, or turning their shoulders to a great part of the audience, besides many other inconveniencies; so that what was conceived would prove a remedy became a very great evil.

Some were of opinion that notwithstanding the largeness of a theatre, its interior formation might greatly contribute to render it commodious for hearing. They tortured their brains not a little to demonstrate such problematic doctrine, but without applying much to geometry for her assistance in their puzzled situation. For the better elucidation of their meaning they made choice of the figure of a bell preferably to all others, and to which they were pleased to give the epithet of phonic.

According to those wiseacres the mouth of the bell answers to the opening of the stage and the middle box is placed where the clapper of a bell is suspended from. It is not difficult to discover how such a notion could be received; it was from the similitude or analogy which unphilosophical heads thought they discovered between the figure of a bell and the sound it gave. But how groundless such reasoning is will readily appear; the concave figure of a bell with its outspreading lips is extremely well fitted for the spreading abroad on every side the sound which the clapper excites by striking on the lips; the bell, being suspended on high, soon throws into agitation the ocean of air that surrounds it. What can be thence inferred? Is it to be expected that the voice of a singer who is placed, as it were, in the mouth of the bell of the stage can cause the like effect in the internal parts of it?

An absurdity of this sort can only be adopted by such understandings as believe that the person who is born under the sign of Aquarius will undergo great perils upon the sea, or by those who against the bite of a serpent prescribe as a sovereign specific the serpentine wood, because it resembles a serpent; with many other inferences equally ridiculous, yet have been esteemed as the legitimate children of analogy when the syllogistic sophistry of the schools had disgraced the name of philosophy. Besides the inconveniencies already recited there are others annexed to the figure of a bell, in the sense those pseudo-connoisseurs would apply it; as the narrowing, in the manner of a bell towards its upper part, the area of the parterre, and thereby screening several boxes from a view of the stage, etc.

Should we perchance be asked, What then is the most commodious shape that can be given to the interior part of a theatre and which of the curve lines is the most eligible for disposing the boxes in the best manner? Our answer is: the same that the ancients made use of in their theatres, the semi-circular.

It is well known that of all the figures of an equal perimeter the circle is that which contains the greatest space. Therefore the spectators placed in a semi-circle are all presented in a like manner towards the stage, of which they have a full view, their hearing and seeing being alike uninterrupted. So true it is that after all the wanderings from art in curious researches, we are often obliged to return to the simple and plain instructions she had delivered to our forefathers. There is one inconveniency which the semi-circle as employed in modern theatres hath, and which proceeds from our stage being built in a different manner from that of the ancients, whereby the opening of it is too large for the side parts of the audience to see well. But the cause of this complaint might be very soon removed. There needs no more than to change the semi-circular into a semi-elliptic form, which comprehends almost the same advantages, and then its minor axis might be the opening of the stage and its larger allotted for the spectators.

There is yet a better manner of arranging the boxes, and for which invention we are indebted to Andrea Sighizzi, the scholar of Brizio and Dentone:[134] he was the predecessor of Bibiena; his method though had been approved and made use of even by them. The plan he followed was that the boxes, according as they were to be removed from the stage towards the bottom of the theatre, should continue gradually rising by some inches one above the other, and gradually receding to the sides by some inches; by which means every box would have a more commodious view of the stage; and the sight of one could not be intercepted by the other, especially if the partition that separates them were made pervious, in a rack-like form, as may be seen in the Formagliari theatre at Bologna, finished in this manner under the direction of Sighizzi.[135]

The boxes, be they ever so well arranged, have yet one fashionable vice to get rid of, viz. those ornamental parts that have too much relievo, too many swellings and sinuous cavities, because the voice by such inequalities is reverberated irregularly and in part lost. For ever be banished from the interior part of a theatre that kind of ornamenting which represents the orders of architecture; a pedantic affectation devolved to us from the fifteenth century; at which period no scrivener's office or even a family cupboard was made without being ridiculously

---

[134] *Il Dentone* was a name given to the Bolognese painter Girolamo Curti (1575-1632). Perhaps Brizio was another painter of the Bolognese school admired by the architect Sighizzi.
[135] Opera was performed at the *Palazzo Formigliari* at Bologna until it was destroyed by fire in 1802. Sighizzi had refurbished it specifically in order to improve spectators' sightlines to the stage.

adorned with all the orders of the Coliseum; but such misplaced decorations are not suitable to a theatre.

The pilasters and columns that are made up to the boxes, as their elevation can be but of a few feet, present a bad appearance; they seem dwindled into pygmies by losing so much of that loftiness and dignity which is their natural right. The ornaments above, although the cornices be architraved, are too high for the size of simple boxes; besides their purpose is nothing more than to separate one range of boxes from another - But this is not all that is exceptionable here; for as to act conformably to the laws of architecture it is necessary to give to the upper ranges a greater air of lightness, what the Italians call *Sveltezza*, than to the inferior; consequently the boxes must be different in height, whence the internal part of the theatre is made like a semi-zone[136] or tower; and thus, without any necessity, the spectators in the uppermost range of boxes are quite thrown out from the point of view, which is settled by the middle box in the first range; or else there will be but few ranges of boxes made, and thereby a great space will be lost.

Let the architect whose province it is to ornament the interior parts of a theatre in a proper manner condescend to take for model a certain species of the grotesque which is yet to be seen in ancient pictures; and also of the Gothic, they being nearly akin; this proposal, we are well aware, will offend over-nice modern ears.

My meaning is that I would have the props of the boxes to be made very slender, having but a small weight to support. Let the ornaments above be narrow and confined, but in all the parts of a light and delicate workmanship. In fine the architect's principal care should be to leave no article unremedied that might any way tend to impede the view: and at the same time to let no gaping chasm appear by any space remaining unoccupied and lost to every serviceable purpose. Let him also contrive that the audience may appear to form a part of the spectacle to each

---

[136] More properly *septizonium*, the best known example of which is the ornamental façade dedicated by the emperor Septimius Severus in A.D. 203 at one corner of the Palatine Hill in Rome. It is a screen, almost like a stage set, consisting of three niches in between colonnades in ascending stages, each one smaller than the one below.

other, ranged as books are in a library. For producing such an effect no better example can be proposed than the theatre of Faunus, admirably designed by Jacobo Torelli,[137] who in the last century, having passed many years of his life in France, was afterwards ennobled by his country.

An architect will find opportunities of displaying his talents and judgment in directing the workmanship as well as the ornamental parts of the boxes and of the rest of the theatre. That artist will justly merit our praise who will order the carving in wood to be light, but with taste at the same time, and he will be indulged in displaying all the pomp and magnificence of his art on the outside, in galleries, niches, balconies etc. I have seen two plans in Italy wherein no article was wanting even for modern dramatic representations, yet all the majesty of the Grecian theatre was preserved.

One of them was the performance of Tommaso Temanza, a man of extraordinary merit; and who by his writings has given new life to Sansovino and Palladio:[138] the other was the production of the Conte Girolamo dal Pozzo, who by his works has revived in Verona, his native country, the grateful memory of Sanmichele.[139] The theatre which was dedicated some years ago in Berlin to Apollo and the Muses[140] does not fall far short of their idea, and is ranked among the first-rate ornaments of that imperial city.

---

[137] Jacopo or Giacomo Torelli (1608-1678), a stage designer, engineer and innovator of theatrical machinery. The theatre of 'Faunus' referred to here is the *Teatro della Fortuna* of 1677 in his native town of Fano, the plan for which was much discussed in treatises on theatre architecture of the 17th and 18th centuries.

[138] Tommaso Temanza (1705-1789), himself an architect responsible *inter alia* for the church of Santa Maria Maddalena in his native Venice, wrote a series of monographs on famous Italian architects including Jacopo Sansovino (1752) and Palladio (1762).

[139] Michele Sanmicheli (1484-1559), architect of Verona, whose work was admired by Count Girolamo dal Pozzo, an antiquarian and member of the *Accademia filharmonica* in Verona in the mid 18th century. Algarotti may be referring to the *Teatro dell'Accademia*, which presented operas from 1722 until its closure in 1873. The more famous *Teatro Filharmonico* in Verona, renowned as one of the most beautiful opera-houses in Italy, was designed by Galli da Bibiena.

[140] Now the *Deutsche Staatsoper unter den Linden*, most classical and attractive of Berlin's opera-houses, built as the Prussian Royal Opera under Frederick the Great and dedicated by him *Apollini et Musis*. The building was designed in Greek style with Corinthian columns and pediment. It was destroyed by Allied bombing in the Second World War but, being considered a showpiece for the régime, was rebuilt in 1955 by the then East German authorities with elaborate wall-paintings and glittering chandeliers.

CONCLUSION

THERE yet remain several articles that might be added to a subject of this nature which is the result of so many different arts, each in itself important, copious and not ignoble. Let it however suffice for me to have pointed out the way thus far, having proposed to myself no other view than to shew the intimate connections that ought to be kept up among the several constituent parts of the musical drama or opera, by which means the effect will be one regular and harmonious *whole*. The doctrine here laid down will be found sufficient whenever it shall be so lucky as to be honoured by the countenance of a sovereign blessed with a refined understanding and delicacy of taste; because through such a wished-for protection may be restored to its ancient rank in the public's esteem a species of scenical exhibition to whose accomplishment and final embellishing all the polite arts emulously concur. Therefore for many other reasons that might be assigned it is an object not unworthy of a place in the attention even of those who govern kingdoms.

At so happy an epoch as that hinted here we should behold the theatres no longer as a place destined for the reception of a tumultuous assembly, but as the meeting of a solemn audience, where an Addison, Dryden, a Dacier, a Muratori, a Gravina, a Marcelli[141] mght be spectators, without the least disparagement to their judgments.

Then would the opera be no longer called an irrational, monstrous and grotesque composition: on the contrary it would display a lively image of the Grecian tragedy in which architecture, poetry, music, dancing and every kind of

---

[141] André Dacier (1651-1722) was a Classical scholar and translator. Ludovico Antonio Muratori (1672-1750), historian of the Middle Ages and librarian of Modena, was a trenchant critic of contemporary music and opera in, for example, his *Della perfetta poesia italiana* of 1706. Gian Vincenzo Gravina (1664-1718), poet and writer on aesthetics, was patron to Metastasio, who inherited his fortune and thus was enabled to establish his own literary career. It was Gravina who changed the name of Pietro Trapassi into the learned Grecized Italian form of Metastasio. By Marcelli Algarotti is probably referring to Benedetto Marcello. These four seem to be chosen as "arbiters of taste" in France and Italy as Addison and Dryden might be supposed to be in England. Algarotti's ideal of a 'solemn audience' might suggest Wagner's festivals at Bayreuth.

theatrical apparatus united their efforts to create an illusion of such resistless power over the human mind that from the combination of a thousand pleasures formed so extraordinary a one as in our world has nothing to equal it.

But since, agreeably to what I have advanced in the beginning of this essay, the drama or poem of an opera is to contain in it every part, the ground work of every beauty; it is upon the well conducting of that the success of the whole must depend[142] - I therefore thought it not unnecessary to give two examples of a drama, according to the manner I have devised. One of them AENEAS IN TROY; the other IPHIGENIA IN AULIS.[143]

The former is but the embryo of a drama, the latter is a finished one.[144]

Aeneas in Troy is little more than the second book of the *Aeneid* of Virgil put into action with some few alterations, in order to make every incident, as it should, refer to Aeneas who is the principal actor in the piece.

---

[142] [Author's note:]
Il faut se rendre à ce palais magique,
Où les beaux vers, la danse, la musique,
L'art de tromper les yeux par les couleurs,
L'art plus heureux de séduire les coeurs,
De ceux plaisirs font un plaisir unique.
'Let us repair to that gay magic temple where the power of verse, of dancing and of music, joined to the sweet embellishments of painting and the delightful art of enchanting hearts, can make such various charms combine to form one blissful scene.' Voltaire, *Le mondain*. [These lines were prefixed as a motto to the later history of Italian opera that appeared in the 1780s by Stefano, or Esteban Arteaga, though they would seem to apply more naturally to the *tragédie lyrique* of composers like Rameau, for whom Voltaire wrote a libretto on the story of Samson (the music, sadly, has been lost). Arteaga, while praising Gluck, deprecated the work of his librettist Calzabigi, who in 1790 wrote a *Risposta* to Arteaga's criticisms.]

[143] [Author's note:] An *Iphigenia in Aulis* has been presented at the theatre royal in Berlin with the greatest applause [music by C. H. Graun, 1731. The libretto on this subject of Apostolo Zeno had long been popular and was set several times over by different composers. In his *Iphigénie en Aulide* Gluck was accused by the Picciniste Jean François de la Harpe of following the pattern of Algarotti's scenario: his own champion, the Academician Jean Baptiste Suard defended him in a letter to Gluck in which he says, 'the plan of your *Iphigénie* ... has nothing, absolutely nothing in common with that of Algarotti, which I have before me and which is simply Racine's plan reduced and cut to the Italian form' (Hedwig and E. H. Müller von Asow, *The Collected Correspondence and Papers of Christoph Willibald Gluck*, tr. Stewart Thomson, London 1962, p.120). Both libretti, of course, share a common ancestry from Racine. Outside of France it is instructive to note that *opere serie* on the same theme continued to be written, including Cherubini's last Italian opera before he left for Paris in 1787.]

[144] The translation omits here a sentence in which Algarotti says that since he had treated of the theme of Iphigenia in French, he has left it in French 'since this language has today become so common that in Europe there is no gentleman who does not know it as well as his own language.'

The other drama, *Iphigenia in Aulis,* is the subject Euripides represented on the Athenian stage, and which in modern times has been transferred from the Grecian to the French theatre by the affecting Muse of the tender Racine.

In some parts of the fable I have followed the ancient poem, in others the modern:[145] assuming to myself the liberty, among other things, of departing occasionally from the one where necessary to render the action quite simple, and from the other to exhibit Iphigenia with a consistency of character suitable to the *costume* of her age and country. For though she hath a fondness for life through that natural sensation common to all, yet as a Grecian princess and daughter of Agamemnon she meets her fate with a becoming fortitude. In my sketch she is not made a timid supplicant from the beginning and by a sudden change at the end entirely the reverse, as Euripides hath drawn her; for which irregular deviation in point of character and palpable violation of the *costume* he was justly censured by Aristotle in his *Art of Poetry*.[146]

Where I have copied Racine I have made use of his diction as far as my abilities would permit. Where I have followed Euripides' plan Brumoy's[147] translation answered my purpose and the more so as I am confident that the Grecian poet himself, had it been his lot to write in French, could not have clothed his sentiments with a happier diction.

What I have added of my own hath been executed in the best manner I could in order to make the whole wear a congenial semblance of style, in order that it should not appear like a piece of mosaic work made partly of stones and partly of glass. My intent in these essays is to enforce by example the doctrine I have delivered and to present it to the reader's eye in a more striking point of light; that

---

[145] In the preface to his play of 1674 Racine explains why he follows a different *dénouement* from that of Euripides, whereby Eriphyle dies in place of Iphigenia; Algarotti reverts to Euripides.

[146] [Author's note:] ῎Εστι δὲ παράδειγμα πονηρίας μὲν ἤθους ... τοῦ δὲ ἀνωμάλου ἡ ἐν Αὐλίδι Ἰφιγένεια, οὐδὲν γὰρ ἔοικεν ἡ ἱκετεύουσα τῇ ὑστέρᾳ. [Aristotle, *Poetics,* ch. 15: 'An illustration of wickedness of character <is Menelaus in *Orestes*>; and of inconsistency in *Iphigenia in Aulis,* for the girl begging for her life does not seem like the later Iphigenia.']

[147] Pierre Brumoy (1688-1742), a Jesuit priest and scholar who translated the Greek tragedies into French. His version, first published in 1730, was translated into English by Mrs. Charlotte Lennox with help from the Earl of Cork and Dr. Johnson and published at London in 1759.

he in consequence may have clearer ideas and form to himself a sounder judgment whether the rules communicated be practicable or not; although at the same time I may perhaps be considered not unlike to that individual who, having composed the best rules imaginable for tactics, yet could not command twenty grenadiers to wheel about to the right.

AENEAS IN TROY

Quaeque ipsa miserrima vidi,
Et quorum pars magna fui. [5f.][148]

THE personages to be represented are Aeneas, Priam, Paris, Anchises, Iulus, Sinon, Pyrrhus, Calchas, Cassandra, Hecuba, Creusa. The choruses are to consist of Trojan men and women, as well as of the deities, both adverse and friendly to Troy.

The scene of the first act exhibits the country adjacent to Troy, the wooden horse on one side. Priam advances from the city at the head of the principal Trojans; celebrates the flight of the Greeks and the deliverance of his kingdom. The old king enjoys a rapturous triumph on beholding the shore cleared of his enemies and their ships; observing - Here the Dolopian camp was pitched; in this place many a battle fought,

- hic saevus tendebat Achilles [29],

and here the fierce Achilles loosed his vengeful ire. Hecuba at these words calls to mind her son Hector, whom Achilles had slain and afterwards dragged his body round the walls of Troy. The chorus comfort her, joining at the same time with Priam to celebrate the flight of the Greeks; of which shameful departure the Horse, consecrated to Minerva, will prove a perpetual monument.

---

[148] 'The most distressing events I myself saw and in which I played a great part' - Aeneas explaining to Dido what he is going to relate of the fall of Troy. Square brackets enclose the line numbers in book II of Virgil's *Aeneid*. Subsequent citations are translated in the text immediately after each quotation. One might compare this synopsis with *La prise de Troie*, the first part of Berlioz' *Les Troyens*, a work very much in the Gluckian tradition of serious French opera. Where Algarotti adheres quite closely to the outline of the action in Virgil, Berlioz adapts it more freely - for example, greatly enlarging the tragic figure of Cassandra into a major character. Algarotti's presaging of the glory of Rome at the conclusion is paralleled by Dido's vision of the eternal city at the end of Berlioz' opera.

In the midst of their song and dance of joy enters Cassandra

Verace sempre, e non creduta mai

announcing always truth, yet never believed. She prophesies that day to be Troy's last and counsels them to plunge the wooden horse into the sea; adding,

... timeo Danaos et dona ferentes [49],[149]

I dread the Greeks, especially when they offer presents. Aeneas accosts her and is of opinion that the horse should be examined, whether any ambush were therein concealed by the Greeks, but he is opposed by many. Priam invokes the tutelary gods of Troy to inspire him for the best, while the rest sacrifice to the river Xanthus and to the nymphs of mount Ida, inviting them to descend and join with Venus to partake of a festive song and choral dance upon the spot where lately Mars enjoyed the cruel sport of war.

In the second act Sinon is brought a prisoner before the king and utters to him that speech in which Virgil, by his harmonious numbers, hath transmitted to us a noble and energetic specimen of Grecian eloquence. In vain doth Aeneas make every effort to oppose the horse's being admitted within the walls of Troy. The art of Sinon finally prevails and vanquishes a people,

Quos neque Tydides, nec Larissaeus Achilles,
Non anni domuere decem, non mille carinae [197f.]:

Whom neither Diomed, nor Larissa's chief, nor ten years' conflict, nor a thousand ships could e'er subdue. Paris, with an instrument of music in his hand, commences an hymn to Venus and Minerva, now reconciled: at the same time part of the city wall is broken down for the easier introduction of the horse, which is drawn within its precincts, amidst songs of joy and festive dances, by the infatuated Trojans;

> *- pueri circum innuptaeque puellae*
> *Sacra canunt, funemque manu contingere gaudent* [238f.];

Their blooming youths and lovely maids sing votive strains around, rejoicing to touch with eager hands the cords that pull it on.

The third act is begun by Aeneas who, roused in the early part of the night from his sleep by a terrifying vision of Hector, repairs to his tomb with presents and offerings, there commiserates the destiny of his country and calls upon the immortal gods to witness that he had done all that was in his power to prevent the fatal horse from being brought within the city. He further entreats the Gods to endow him with a courage like to that of Hector, when he set fire to the Grecian ships, in order that if his country be doomed to fall, it may not fall unrevenged. He then shapes his course to Priam's palace.

The scene changes to an ample area before the temple of Pallas, where the horse is lodged as a sacred deposit. Sinon relates to Calchas and Pyrrhus (come from within the horse) how his fine-laid scheme had like to have miscarried through the opposition of Aeneas: when he remonstrates that one of the first and most necessary articles to be done for the insuring success is to dispatch Aeneas, being since Hector's death the bravest warrior Troy can boast of. During this speech the Grecians are seen to descend from the horse.

Calchas animates them in a few words to destroy the hostile city; then commences a cantata in a low voice, to which the Greeks answer also in the same way. About the end of the chorus a battle is begun at the bottom of the stage between the guards of the citadel and some Grecians descended from the horse, who want to make themselves masters of the fort. The tumult increases by the

---

[149] In the *Aeneid* it is in fact Laocoön who speaks this famous line.

arrival of the Grecian troops from without the city. Calchas and Sinon, at the front of the stage, pray in a loud voice. And at certain intervals the cries, the groans and lamentations of people wounded and expiring are made to concert with their songs.

The scene of the fourth act is in the courtyard of Priam's palace.

Aedibus in mediis, nudoque sub aetheris axe
Ingens ara fuit, iuxtaque veterrima laurus,
Incumbens arae, atque umbra complexa Penates [512-4]:

In the midst of the imperial edifice, and under the open air, stands a great altar; next to it a laurel tree leaning upon the shrine, and with its foliage hospitably embracing the household gods. There afflicted Hecuba is seen with some Trojan dames, who, all fearful and suppliant, clasp the statues of the gods. Old Priam comes on at one side of the stage, scarce able to walk, being whelmed under an unwieldy weight of armour, which vainly he would put on. Hecuba no sooner sees than she hastes to place him in the consecrated seat near the altar and thus addresses him:

- Quae mens tam dira, miserrime coniux,
Impuli his cingi telis? aut quo ruis? -
Non tali auxilio, nec defensoribus istis
Tempus eget [519-22];

Unhappy husband, what fatal resolution hath impelled you to be thus clothed in armour, or whether do you rush? Alas, the present calamity requires not such assistance as thine, nor so unavailing a defence. For if Troy can yet be saved, it must be by Aeneas' valour only, who now defends the tower of the palace and by the slaughter of so many Greeks hath in part avenged the havoc of his country.

One of the principal Trojan dames remarks how much more advantageous it might have proved to pay a proper attention to the advice of Aeneas and the prophecy of Cassandra. On the instant a tremendous noise is heard of the tower falling to the ground. Hecuba begins a prayer to the gods, in which she beseeches them to preserve from captivity the concubines of Priam and his queen. - The other women have hardly time to reassume the votive strain when Pyrrhus enters, pursuing Polites, who falls dead at his father's feet. Next follows the speech of Priam, strongly accompanied.[150] Then the distressed old king

*- telum imbelle sine ictu
Conjicit* [544f.],

Lets fly a weak and ineffectual arrow at Pyrrhus; who replies according to the words in Virgil and kills the aged monarch. The women fill the air with shrieks; Pyrrhus orders them to be conducted to the ships of Greece and goes off in quest of Aeneas. The Trojan prince enters from the opposite side of the stage, and descrying Priam slain makes a short lamentation over him,

Haec finis Priami fatorum – [554]

such is the end of Priam's fate. And straight bethinks him of his own aged sire, Anchises, and his young son Iulus. But having formed a resolution to perish with his country and to wreak some share of vengeance either on Helen or on Sinon, his mother Venus appears and shews to him the adverse deities to Troy, all zealously confederated in its overthrow. - Aeneas being gone off the stage, a chorus succeeds by those deities and a ballet by furies.

In the fifth act is introduced in the residence of Aeneas that noble contention, so masterly expressed by Virgil, between Anchises, determined to expire with Troy,

---

[150] In this scenario Algarotti makes a few suggestions for the musical setting, here perhaps an accompanied recitative for the aged Priam's plea to the young warrior Pyrrhus.

and his son Aeneas, resolved to snatch him from falling into the hands of the Grecian spoilers. Not being able to prevail, he resumes his arms to sally out again among the Greeks, but as Creusa and Iulus lay hold on Aeneas to stop him, a sudden miraculous flame descends from heaven and plays inoffensively round the head of little Iulus. Thunder is heard on the left side! Stricken with such admonitions from above, Anchises consents at last to depart.

The scene changes and presents the horrible view of a dismantled city, half of it a prey to flames;

- humi fumat Neptunia Troia [*Aeneid* III.3],

Troy, which Neptune built, now smokes upon the ground. The chorus here is to consist of Trojans deploring their calamity; and of Grecians insulting them as they march; the Coryphaeus is cruel Calchas.

As soon as the stage is cleared Aeneas enters, seeking for and calling Creusa, who in the flight had lost her way. Her ghost appears to him and foretells first his destined wanderings on the sea, and next his founding a new empire: at that word through the smoke of Troy must be seen to blaze forth, with resplended glory, the capitol. Immediately follows a chorus of deities, and a ballet by Rome's protecting genii.

IPHIGENIA IN AULIS[151]

---

[151] Algarotti's French libretto is presented here side by side with the contemporary English translation. It will be noticed that the latter occasionally varies or embroiders on the French original. A small number of lines is missing in the translation: their sense is supplied in square [ ] brackets.

Not only did Algarotti conceive the libretto in French, but he clearly follows the form of the *tragédie lyrique*. The dialogue in prose would have been delivered musically as accompanied recitative (*récit*). Occasional extended soliloquys suggest a more *arioso* style of recitative, but the number of set *airs* is small in comparison with *opera seria*, one only in both Acts 4 and 5. Act 3 has the largest number with three *airs*, beginning, unusually, with an *air* for Agamemnon, its placing and import reminiscent of Armide's *Ah, si la liberté* at the start of Act 3 of Gluck's opera. The *airs* are all single verses of five or six lines, with the one exception of Iphigenia's *Que je meure obéissante* in Act 3. Its two verses of six and four lines respectively may imply a *da capo* aria, unusual in *tragédie lyrique*, but apt here perhaps by reason of the climactic significance of this *air*, Iphigenia pleading the effects of her threatened death for herself (in verse 1) and for her family, country and lover (middle section - verse 2), before returning to herself (repeat of verse 1).

As well as the *récit* and *airs* there are three concerted numbers: a duet for Agamemnon and Ulysses in Act 1, a duet of mutual incomprehension for Agamemnon and Iphigenia in Act 2 and a quartet of conflicting emotions in Act 4, the four characters eventually concurring in their different ways: *Dieux! quelle est donc votre cruauté!* There are a few other musical indications in the text, one of them being a short *symphonie pathétique* at the start of Act 4.

Apart from the simplicity of the *airs* the other major French feature is the extended *divertissement* with chorus and ballet that ends each act. In Act 1 it is the women who accompany the arrival of Clytemnestra and Iphigenia, the first time women's voices would be heard in the opera, and in Act 2 praise of the merits of Achilles who is to marry Iphigenia. Act 3 ends with a scene in the temple of Diana, where the goddess, invoked by the priest Calchas, pronounces through an oracle that it is Iphigenia who must be sacrificed so that the Greek army may proceed to Troy. The chorus is intercut with Calchas seeking to reassure Agamemnon, who can scarcely find words to express his torment. Act 4 ends with lamentations at the fate of Iphigenia, while in Act 5 the *divertissement* expands to fill virtually the entire act as the sacrifice goes ahead. Calchas is raising his knife to slay Iphigenia when Diana appears, *dea ex machina*, to save Iphigenia and claim her as her own, substituting a sacrificial deer for the girl. All proclaim a miracle and as the goddess is now appeased the long delayed winds begin to blow for the Greek ships to sail against Troy. An antiphonal chorus of soldiers on land and sailors on board ship and a dance of sailors conclude the opera.

It is, of course, difficult to estimate how effective the libretto might be in any musical setting. What can be said is that Algarotti has convincingly laid out the development of the story and given opportunities for a composer to explore the varied emotions of the principal characters - Agamemnon, Iphigenia, Clytemnestra and Achilles - with substantial roles also for Ulysses, the voice of the Greek forces determined to seek revenge on Troy, and the priest Calchas, while also providing for a lively and diverse spectacle in the *divertissements*: more decorative at first in Acts 1 and 2, these become integrated into the dramatic texture as the opera progresses. The interplay between the personal emotions of the individual characters and the wider political context in which they are set, moving from the enclosed scene of Agamemnon and his confidant Arcas at the outset into the public arena of the sacrifice at the close, is well handled by Algarotti. The libretto certainly allows one to imagine the type of opera that his essay advocates: for a musical realisation of that type we must turn to Gluck.

IPHIGÉNIE EN AULIDE	IPHIGENIA IN AULIS
OPÉRA	AN OPERA
quot victimae in una!	'How many victims in one!'

ACTEURS	The PERSONAGES
AGAMEMNON	AGAMEMNON
ACHILLE	ACHILLES
ULYSSE	ULYSSES
CLYTEMNESTRE femme d'Agamemnon	CLYTEMNESTRA, wife of Agamemnon
IPHIGÉNIE fille d'Agamemnon	IPHIGENIA, daughter of Agamemnon
CALCHAS grand Prêtre	CALCHAS, high priest
ARCAS domestique d'Agamemnon	ARCAS, one of Agamemnon's household officers
TROUPE de Soldats d'Agamemnon	A BAND of soldiers belonging to Agamemnon
TROUPE de filles Grecques	A BAND of Grecian nymphs
TROUPE de filles consacrées à Diane	A BAND of virgins consecrated to Diana
TROUPE de Prêtres	A BAND of priests
TROUPE d'Esclaves, de Captives et de Soldats d'Achille	A BAND of slaves and soldiers belonging to Achilles

ACTE I

Le Théâtre représente le camp des Grecs près de la ville d'Aulide. La flotte Grecque paraît sur la mer dans le fond. Sur le devant on voit l'entrée de la tente d'Agamemnon. Le Théâtre est d'abord sombre, et s'éclaire peu à peu.

SCÈNE I
AGAMEMNON et ARCAS

AGAMEMNON
Viens, Arcas, suis-moi.

ARCAS
Quoi, Seigneur, vous devancez l'Aurore!
Vos yeux seuls sont ouverts,
tandis que les oiseaux, les vents et l'Euripe,
tandis que tout encore est dans le silence.

AGAMEMNON
Heureux ceux qui loin des honneurs
vivent sans gloire et sans soucis!

ARCAS
Agamemnon issu du sang de Jupiter,
à la tête de l'armée, de vingt rois,
et de mille vaisseaux
que la Grèce a assemblés contre l'Asie,
depuis quand tenez-vous ce langage?
Père de la belle Iphigénie,
Achille fils d'une Déesse,
le plus vaillant des Grecs,
celui qui doit renverser la superbe Troye,
Achille recherche en mariage cette fille.
Que vous reste-t-il à demander aux Dieux? Il est vrai
qu'un long calme ... mais hélas! quels pleurs
vois-je couler de vos yeux attachés sur ce billet?

ACT I

The theatre represents the Grecian camp near the city of Aulis A fleet of ships is seen at the bottom of the stage. On the front part of it is the entrance to the royal tent of Agamemnon. The theatre, dark at first, becomes gradually enlightened.

SCENE I
AGAMEMNON, ARCAS

AGAMEMNON
Come, Arcas, haste; obey your sovereign's call.

ARCAS
Why thus, great king, forerun the morning's dawn?
No eyes but yours in Aulis do yet wake;
The birds, the winds, the Euripus is still,
An universal silence reigns o'er all.

AGAMEMNON
Happy who, far from glory and renown,
Nor know their splendour nor the cares annexed.

ARCAS
Can Agamemnon, sprung from thundering Jove,
Chief of our army, first of twenty kings,
Supreme commander of a thousand ships,
By leagued Greece 'gainst Asia's shore employed,
Speak such desponding words as those I've heard?
Fair Iphigenia is your lovely daughter,
And her Achilles (of a goddess born,
The foremost hero of our Grecian bands,
By fate appointed Ilion to destroy)
Woos for his wife and hopes for your consent.
What other boon have you from heaven to wish?
'Tis true that long suspended by a calm -
But ha! what tears gush from your royal eyes!

Pleurez-vous d'Oreste,
Clytemnestre ou la belle Iphigénie?

AGAMEMNON
Non, tu ne mourras point; je n'y saurais consentir.

ARCAS
Seigneur ...

AGAMEMNON
Tu sais qu'il y a trois mois que nous étions prêts
à faire voile de l'Aulide, lorsque ce calme que nous y
retient encore nous ferma le chemin de Troye.
Frappé de ce prodige j'interrogai Calchas.
Il consulta Diane
qu'on adore dans ces lieux.
Mais que deviens-je, Arcas,
lorsqu'on me répondit
que pour ouvrir le chemin de Troye
il fallait sacrifier Iphigénie.

ARCAS
Votre fille!

AGAMEMNON
Que te dirai-je, Arcas?
Victime de l'ambition et pressé par Ulysse,
je consentis après milles combats à sacrifier ma fille.
Mais quel artifice a-t-il fallu chercher
pour l'arracher des bras d'une mère?
J'empruntai le langage d'Achille son amant.
J'écrivis en Argos qu'il ne voulait partir pour Troye
que l'hymen n'eut couronné ses feux.

ARCAS
Et croyez-vous, Seigner, que le bouillant Achille
souffrira qu'on abuse de son nom et ne volera pas
à la vengeance?

AGAMEMNON
Il était absent alors. Tu te souviens que Pélée son
père, assailli dans son proper royaume, l'avait
rappellé. On aurait cru que cette expedition
du le retenir longtemps.
Mais qui peut résister
à ce foudre de guerre?

Il se monstra, vainquit,
et hier il revint en Aulide. Mais de plus puissants
soifs me retiennent. Moi, je serai bourreau d'une
fille, que le sang, la jeunesse, sa tendresse pour moi
et mille vertus me rendent sacrée!
Non, les Dieux ne'approuveraient pas ce sacrifice.
Ils ont voulu seulement m'éprouver,
et me condamneraient, si je leur livrais
la victime qu'ils demandent.
Arcas, cours au devant de la Reine;
rends-lui ce billet, et que tes discours s'accordent
avec ce que j'écris.
Je lui mande, qu'Achille, ne soupirant qu'après la

Weep you for the loss of young Orestes?
Your queen expired, or Iphigenia dead?

AGAMEMNON
Thou shall not die; I never will consent.

ARCAS
Dread sir ...

AGAMEMNON
- Thou know'st three months are now elapsed
Since by this calm, which still detains us here,
We were impeded in our course to Troy.
Struck at the portent, I summoned Calchas
To learn the cause. He to Diana's shrine
(The goddess here adored) devote repaired.
But oh! what racking agonies I felt,
When he brought answer back that the pure blood
Of Iphigenia sacrificed - (my child!)
Was the price destined for the fall of Troy.

ARCAS
To sacrifice your child! -

AGAMEMNON
Even so, good Arcas,
Urged by ambition and Ulysses' wiles,
'Gainst nature's voice I did consent. -
But then what scheme, what artifice to use
To draw the daughter from the mother's arms!
All would prove vain, 'till in Achilles' name
To wed the princess, hither she's invited
With Clytemnestra to behold the rites.

ARCAS
Think you, sir, the haughty proud Achilles
Will tamely bear to have his name abused?

AGAMEMNON
He then was far from Aulis and from me,
His father Peleus' realm from hostile troops
To guard; we believed so glorious an exploit
Would fill up all his soul; nor let him think
Of us till that were over; which some time
Must keep him occupied: but his dread sword
What power can long resist? At his approach
Far fled the foe. - He marched, he saw, he
And to our camp did yesterday return. [vanquished;
Guess my confusion; - but that is not all. -
A father's feelings for a favourite child
Harrow my heart, nor can my eyes know rest.
Sure heaven can't countenance a crime like this.
'Tis only meant to try how I should bear,
Submissive to its will, so dire a blow.
But thou chosen confidant of what I feel,
Fly with this letter, intercept their coming;
On that depends my Iphigenia's life -
Join with the contents I have written;
Tell 'em Achilles, lukewarm in his love,

gloire, veut différer cet hymen jusqu'à son retour
de Troye. Va, cours, prends un guide fidèle.
Si ma fille met le pied dans l'Aulide, elle est morte.
Sauve-la d'Ulysse, de l'armée, de Calchas,
de la Religion; sauve-la de ma propre faiblesse.

ARCAS
Comptez sur moi, Seigneur, je vole pour vous obéir.

AGAMEMNON
AIR
Suspend ta colère,
ô chaste Déesse,
ne souille pas tes autels
du sang d'une mortelle,
qui a toujours suivi tes lois ...

Mais on entre. C'est Achille:
Dieux! Ulysse le suit.

SCÈNE II
AGAMEMNON, ACHILLE, ULYSSE

AGAMEMNON
Quoi, seigneur, se peut-il que vos triomphes soient
si grands et si rapides! La Victoire vous a précédé
dans la Thessalie, et vous suivez de près la
Renommée dans l'Aulide. Presqu'en passant
vous soumîtes Lesbos, la plus puissante alliée
des Troyens; et ces grands exploits ne sont que
les amusements d'Achille oisif.

ACHILLE
Seigneur, puisse bientôt le Ciel qui nous arrête
ouvrir un champ plus noble à mes destinés!
Mais que me faut-il croire d'un bruit
qui me surprend, et me met au comble
de mes voeux?
On dit qu'Iphigénie
va bientôt arriver en ces lieux,
et que je vais être le plus heureux des mortels.

AGAMEMNON
Ma fille! Qui vous a dit qu'elle doit arriver?

ACHILLE
Qu'à donc ce bruit qui doive vous étonner?

AGAMEMNON (*à Ulysse*)
Ciel, saurait-il mon sacrifice!

ULYSSE
Agamemnon s'étonne avec raison.
Quoi! tandis que le Ciel
est en courroux contre les Grecs,
qu'il faut fléchir les Dieux,
qu'il leur faut du sang,
et peut-être du plus précieux, Achille,
le seul Achille ne songe qu'à l'amour.

Defers to wed 'till Troy be overthrown. -
If she to Aulis, she dies. – Ulysses,
Calchas and the assembled Greeks will all
Demand her virgin blood. – Speed, Arcas, speed,
Save her from them and from a father's weakness.

ARCAS
With wings of zeal I'll execute your will. (*Exit.*

AGAMEMNON
AIR
Say, Diana, goddess bright,
Can you such an act endure,
As to shock your heavenly sight
With blood royal, chaste and pure.

But hark! - a noise as of approaching feet. -
Achilles, Gods! - with him fell Ulysses.

SCENE II
AGAMEMNON, ACHILLES, ULYSSES

AGAMEMNON
Amazing, sir, the conquest you have made!
With victory in my word a nobler field
And (fame your herald) now return to Aulis.
Lesbos, the strongest city that's allied
To perjured Troy you vanquished in your way,
To save your native Thessaly from havoc.
Exploits like these to you are but amusements.

ACHILLES
May heaven, great monarch, friendly to our wishes,
Soon open to my word a nobler field
For glorious deeds. – But first let me express
The joy with which my raptured bosom glows,
On hearing a report which glads my soul
That I'm to wed your daughter, and that soon
Ev'n here in Aulis Hymen will unite us
And render me the happiest of men.

AGAMEMNON
Who told you, prince, that Iphigenia comes?

ACHILLES
Why thus alarmed? Can such news then bode ill?

AGAMEMNON (*aside to Ulysses*)
Think you he knows the stratagem we've used?

ULYSSES
Not without reason Agamemnon wonders,
Illustrious hero, that while adverse heaven
Opposes our intent, and the angry gods
Are, by the effusion of most precious blood,
To be prevailed on to espouse our cause,
You think of nothing but the joys of love
And clasping Iphigenia in your arms.

ACHILLE

Dans les champs de Troye les efforts seront voir
qui chérit plus la gloire ou d'Ulysse, ou de moi.
Vous pouvez maintenant à loisir
consulter les victimes sur le silence des vents.
Moi, qui de ce soin me repose sur Calchas,
souffrez, Seigneur, que je presse un hymen
dont dépend mon bonheur.
Je saurai bien réparer
devant Troye les moments
que l'amour me demande en Aulide.

AGAMEMNON

Ô Ciel, pourquoi faut-il que tu fermes le chemin
de l'Asie à de tels Héros?
N'aurais-je vu tant de valeur, que pour m'en
retourner avec plus de confusion!

ULYSSE

Dieux, qu'entends-je!

ACHILLE
Qu'osez-vous dire?

AGAMEMNON

Qu'il faut abandonner notre enterprise. Les vents
nous sont refusé: Le Ciel protège Troye, les Dieux
par trop de présages se déclarent en sa faveur.

ACHILLE

Quels sont donc ces présages?

AGAMEMNON

Vous-même, Seigneur, souvenez-vous de ce que
les Oracles ont prédit de vous.

ACHILLE

Les Parques, il est vrai, ont prédit à ma mère,
que je pouvais choisir
d'une vie longue et sans gloire,
ou de peu de jours suivis d'une gloire immortelle:
Achille n'a pas balancé. Couronné par l'hymen
je cours à Troye. J'y mourrai;
mais ne mourrai pas tout entier.

AIR

Les cris des Troyennes
répéteront mon nom,
reconnaissent mes coups
dans les blessures de leurs époux:
Et le nom d'Achille sera l'entretien
des siècles à venir.

SCÈNE III
AGAMEMNON & ULYSSE

AGAMEMNON
Hélas!

ACHILLES

My deeds among Troy's sons shall soon declare,
Who pants for glory more, or thou or I;
I born of Thetis, thou Laertes' son.
I leave to you political intrigues,
Or talk inglorious of consulting entrails
And slaughtered victims why the winds are dumb.
But think not, sir, (*to Agam.*) the nuptials I solicit
Will in the least abate my thirst of fame.
No – the few hours I may here give to love
Troy shall repay with measure of revenge.

AGAMEMNON

Why, cruel heaven, debar our way to Troy?
Have I then seen so many heroes met
But to lament their disappointed hopes
And all, with shame oppressed, return to Greece?

ULYSSES

What have I heard our sovereign say!

ACHILLES
Great king,
You mean not sure as you have spoke!

AGAMEMNON
Too true:
Heaven's partial favour has for Troy declared,
By various presages in its behalf.

ACHILLES

What various presages? I've heard of none!

AGAMEMNON

Remember, sir, concerning thy own life
What in clear terms the oracle foretold.

ACHILLES

I do remember well the fates' decree,
As by the answer to my mother given,
That I enjoy a short but glorious life,
Or without fame drag on chain of years.   [love;
The choice I've made shall now be crowned with
And then from Troy new laurels shall I reap,
Or, if there fall, my fame will ever flourish.

AIR

The Trojan dames with plaintive cries
Shall oft repeat my name;
While, from their wounded, groans arise,
And give me deathless fame.

SCENE III
AGAMEMNON, ULYSSES

AGAMEMNON
O, what cruel conflict tears my breast!

ULYSSE
Achille, Seigneur, aurait-il changé vos desseins?

AGAMEMNON
Ni Achille, ni Ajax, ni Diomède, ni tous les Rois
qui sont dans l'armée ne pouraient faire changer
un dessin qu'Agamemnon aurait pris.

ULYSSE
Que faut-il donc que j'augure de ces soupirs et de
vos discours? Une nuit a ébranlé votre constance
et détruit l'ouvrage de tant de jours.

AGAMEMNON
Non, Seigneur, je ne saurais croire que les Dieux
demandent une telle victoire.

ULYSSE
Que dites-vous, Seigneur?
Calchas nous a expliqué clairement
les ordres des Dieux; lui qui est le
dépositaire et l'interprète fidèle de leurs secrets.

AGAMEMNON
Les ordres des Dieux sont obscurs, et souvent
impénétrables aux mortels.

ULYSSE
Quoi, Seigneur, vous devez votre fille à la Grèce;
vous nous l'avez promise. Mais que dis-je à la
Grèce? Vous la devez à vous-même. Et pour qui
donc allons nous courir aux campagnes de Xanthe,
pour qui abandonnons-nous nos femmes, nos
enfants, nos royaumes, si ce n'est pour venger la
honte des Atrides? Votre voix pressante nous a
assemblé, les suffrages de vingt Rois, qui pouvaient
tous vous disputer le rang suprême, vous ont mis
à la tête de cette armée. Et le premier ordre du
Général est de refuser la victoire; le premier conseil
du Chef de la Grèce est de renvoyer les Grecs qu'il
a assemblés.

AGAMEMNON
Ah, Seigneur, que loin du malheur qui m'accable,
vous vous montrez aisément, magnanime. Mais si
vous entendiez condamner votre fils Télémaque,
s'il devait approcher de l'autel ceint de fatal
bandeau, vous changeriez de langage, vous croiriez
moins les Oracles: Je vous verrais courir et vous
jeter contre Calchas et lui.

DUO
AGAMEMNON
   Voyez ma fille expirante
   entre les sanglots et les larmes
   verser son sang innocent
   sous un couteau impie.
   Que la piété de père
   attendrisse votre âme.

ULYSSES
Is it Achilles can have wrought this change?

AGAMEMNON
Nor he, nor Ajax, Diomed, nor all
The kings, combined in this war 'gainst Troy,
Could Agamemnon force to change resolves.

ULYSSES
What must I now conclude these smothered sighs
And speech ambiguous can pretend? has then
One night o'erturned the work of many days?

AGAMEMNON
Not so, Ulysses; but my heart can't believe
That gracious heaven commands to slay a child.

ULYSSES
I know not Agamamnon in these words.
Has not the avowed interpreter of Gods,
Calchas, to whom the will of heaven is known,
Declared in terms that leave no room to doubt?

AGAMEMNON
Perplexed and intricate are heavenly mandates,
And oft superior to the reach of mortals.

ULYSSES
Remember, sir, you owe your child to Greece,
Your word is given – Why did I say to Greece?
To your own house's fame you owe her blood.
Is't not to avenge the insult it received
The Grecian kings assemble on this shore.
Who called us hither? You, now raised above
Your fellow sovereigns, their chief elect,
Shall it be said your general's first command
Was to dismiss so great a league inglorious
And shrink supinely from the talk of honour;
Turning our backs on victory that woos
To certain conquest and immortal fame.

AGAMEMNON
You talk it nobly, sir; but were your son,
Telemachus, like Iphigenia doomed;
Were you to see him at the altar placed,
The sacred fillet round his temples bound,
His bosom bared for the executive blow,
Like me you'd doubt the oracle's decree
And, to protect, rush between him and Calchas.

DUO
AGAMEMNON
   Behold my child, breathless lying,
   What plaints, what tears, what groans!
   View a wretched mother sighing;
   Such precious blood a people moans.
   Let a father's feelings move you.

ULYSSE
Voyez le superbe Troye,
parmi mes chants de victoire,
plongée dans les flammes
sous nos flambeaux vengeurs.
Que les sentiments du Héros
triomphent dans votre coeur.

AGAMEMNON
Eh bien, Seigneur, j'ai donné ma parole; et si ma fille vient, je consens qu'elle périsse. Mais si, malgré mes soins, son destin heureux la retient dans Argos, ou bien l'arrête en chemin; souffrez que j'explique cet obstacle comme un arrêt du Ciel, et que j'accepte le secours de quelque Dieu favorable, que sa piété, son innocence et son âge auront interessé à mon salut …
Mais quels sons frappent mon oreille?
(*On entend de loin une simphonie guerrière, et l'on voit paraître sur un char Clytemnestre, et Iphigénie accompagnées de femmes Grecques, et de Soldats, qui les ont reçues à l'entrée du Camp.*)

Dieux! c'est elle-même.
Dans l'état où je suis
je me dérobe à ce funeste spectacle.

SCÈNE IV
ULYSSE, CLYTEMNESTRE, IPHIGÉNIE et le CHOEUR

CHOEUR
Non, la belle Hélène,
que l'insolent Pâris a enlevé à Ménélas,
n'était pas plus belle qu'Iphigénie,
que l'hymen doit unir au vaillant Achille.

(*Tandis que le Choeur chante Clytemnestre et Iphigénie descendent du char, aidées des femmes Grecques.*)

ULYSSE
Venez, et que l'appareil de ce Camp
n'effraye point vos yeuz.

CLYTEMNESTRE
Mes yeux cherchent en vain Agamemnon,
qu'ils auraient du voir le premier.

IPHIGÉNIE
Quel malheur, hélas, le retient éloigné de nous?
Serait-ce, Madame, que nous serions arrivées
contre son gré?

ULYSSE
Les soins de l'armée
le dérobent un moment à votre vue.
Mais vous, Iphigénie, venez,
montrez-vous aux Soldats

ULYSSES
Behold proud Troy, vanquished lying,
What plaints, what tears, what groans!
View a prostrate people sighing,
There's martial music in their moans.
Let a hero's feelings prove you.

AGAMEMNON
Be't so, our royal promise to devote
My child is given; let unrelenting fate
Have the completion of its dire decree,
But if my Iphigenia's better stars
Prevent her coming to unhallowed Aulis,
Then be it construed in the princess' favour
That heaven has changed, and thirsts not for
    her blood.
What sprightly sounds invade my startled ear?
(*A warlike symphony is heard at a distance; Clytemnestra and Iphigenia are drawn forward in a triumphal car, attended by Grecian women and the guards who receive them on their entrance to the camp.*)
My queen and daughter in the camp arrived!
Gods, 'tis too much: I cannot bear their sight
And fly with horror from an interview.

SCENE IV
ULYSSES, CLYTEMNESTRA, IPHGENIA, and the CHORUS.

CHORUS
Not the famed Helen, won by Paris,
As beauteous Iphigenia fair is,
And now she comes to wed Achilles;
Of gods consenting such the will is.

(*While the chorus sing Clytemnestra and Iphigenia descend from the car, assisted by the Grecian women.*)

ULYSSES
Advance, bright dames; let not the pomp of war
Or sight unusual of any army fright ye.

CLYTEMNESTRA
My eyes in vain for Agamemnon seek;
He should be first to meet us on arriving.

IPHIGENIA
Some luckless accident detains him from us.
[Could it be, Madam, that we have come here against his will?]

ULYSSES
The weighty cares attendant on his rank
May for some moments keep him from your sight.
Meanwhile do you fair Iphigenia come,
And shew your beauty to the Grecian troops

comme un Astre favorable au salut de la Grèce.

CHOEUR
Non, la belle Hélène,
que l'insolent Pâris a enlevé à Ménélas,
n'était pas plus belle qu'Iphigénie,
que l'hymen doit unir au vaillant Achille.

Un d'entre le Choeur
Comme l'étoile du matin brille
parmi les feuillages épais d'une forêt,
telle est Iphigénie parmi les lances
et les javelets de cette armée.

(Les chants seront entremêlés de danse, qui sera composée de femmes Grecques et de Soldats.)

Un autre d'entre le Choeur
Père fortuné, heureuse mère,
à qui la belle Iphigénie a souri
en voyant la clarté du jour!

Deux d'entre le Choeur
Achille plus heureux encore,
entre les bras de qui elle va verser
des larmes dans l'ombre de la nuit!

CHOEUR
Non, la belle Hélène,
que l'insolent Pâris a enlevé à Ménélas,
n'était pas plus belle qu'Iphigénie,
que l'hymen doit unir au vaillant Achille.

(On danse.)

ACTE II

Le Théâtre représente une Colonnade, au travers de laquelle on voit des Jardins.

SCÈNE I
AGAMEMNON seul
Ciel! Arcas a manqué le chemin d'Argos,
et la colère des Dieux
a confondu toute ma prudence!
Ô jour fatal! ma fille est arrivée.
Je vois Ulysse et Ménélas, je vois déjà Calchas
me la demander au nom de la Grèce
et des Dieux.
Mais, Ciel! La voici elle-même, évitons-la.

As a kind star, propitious to our league.

CHORUS
Not the famed Helen, won by Paris,
As beauteous Iphigenia fair is,
And now she comes to wed Achilles;
Of gods consenting such the will is.

One of the CHORUS
As the bright morning star pervades
Of leafy groves the verdant shades;
So in the midst of Grecian arms
Beam kindly Iphigenia's charms.

(The song is mixed with dancing by the Greek women and the Soldiers.)

Another of the CHORUS
Hail, happy mother, happy sire,
Still blest be that auspicious morn;
The princess smiled as she was born;
For her our zealous vows conspire.

Two of the CHORUS
Achilles, first of human race,
What a sweet treasure you'll embrace!
While all her beauties veiled by night,
She yields you rapturous delight.

CHORUS
Not the famed Helen, won by Paris,
As beauteous Iphigenia fair is,
And now she comes to wed Achilles;
Of gods consenting such the will is.

A DANCE.

ACT II

The theatre represents a colonnade, through which gardens are seen.

SCENE I
AGAMEMNON alone
What stroke of adverse fortune has contrived
That faithful Arcas should mistake his way?
In what have I deserved the wrath of heaven?
To me this day is big with misery.
I hear Ulysses, Calchas, Menelaus
Demand, both in the name of Greece and heaven,
My child for victim - She comes - What a meeting!
Hold, heart - I fain would shun her, but I can't.

SCÈNE II
AGAMEMON & IPHIGÉNIE

IPHIGÉNIE
Seigneur, quoi vous me fuyez? Eh quels soins
vous dérobent si tôt à votre fille?
Mon respect tantôt a fait place
aux transports de la Reine.
Ne puis-je vous arrêter un moment à mon tour?
ne puis-je? ...

AGAMEMNON
Eh bien, embrassez votre père, ma fille;
Il vous aime toujours.

IPHIGÉNIE
Que cet amour me comble de joie!
Quel plaisir de vous contempler dans ce nouvel
éclat, couronné de gloire et d'honneurs!

AGAMEMNON
Vous méritiez un père plus heureux.

IPHIGÉNIE
Quel félicité peut vous manquer? J'ai cru n'avoir
que des grâces à rendre au Ciel.

AGAMEMNON (à part)
Grands Dieux, dois-je la préparer à son malheur!

IPHIGÉNIE
Seigneur, vous vous cachez et semblez soupirer.
Tous vos regards ne tombent
qu'avec peine sur moi.
Aurions-nous abandonné Argos sans votre ordre?

AGAMEMNON
Hélas; ma fille, je vous vois toujours des mêmes
yeux. Mais le temps aussi bien que lieux
sont changé. Ma joie est combattue ici
par de cruels soins.

IPHIGÉNIE
Ah, mon père, que votre rang soit oublié
à ma vue. Que je retrouve encore en vous
ces soins, cette tendresse que vous aviez pour moi.
On dit que Calchas va offrir aux Dieux
un sacrifice solennel.

AGAMEMNON
Dieux cruels! (à part)

IPHIGÉNIE
Me sera-t-il permis, Seigneur, de me joindre
à vos voeux? La Grèce verra-t-elle à l'autel
votre heureuse famille?

AGAMEMNON
Hélas!

SCENE II
AGAMEMNON, IPHIGENIA

IPHIGENIA
Why, sir, avoid the presence of your child?
There was a time you would not slight me thus.
What mighty cares have from me weaned your heart?
As duty urged I yielded to the queen
The first occasion of embracing you,
Now in my turn I hope to share that favour.

AGAMEMNON
Come to your father's arms, never more fond.

IPHIGENIA
Transporting news! – My bosom bounds with joy!
What ecstasy to see you now supreme
O'er all the Grecian sovereigns here assembled!

AGAMEMNON
Your innocence deserves a better father.

IPHIGENIA
A better cannot be; for which kind heaven
Receives my constant and most grateful thanks.

AGAMEMNON (aside)
How let her know the secret of her fate!

IPHIGENIA
There's something labouring in your breast: those
You fain would smother but confirm it more.   [sighs
'Tis with anxiety you look on me.
Are we from Argos come without your order?

AGAMEMNON
Alas! mistake me not. Your father's eyes
With the same wonted tenderness behold you.
But such eventful changes have ta'en place
The joy of seeing you is dashed with sorrow.

IPHIGENIA
Forget a moment your superior rank
In a child's presence – be my father still,
Nor blush to see me happy in your kindness.
'Tis said, sir, that a solemn sacrifice
By Calchas to the heavenly powers anon
Is to be made.

AGAMEMNON
Heart-rending question!

IPHIGENIA
Will you indulge me to be present, sir,
And join the general prayer for your success?
The Greeks would wonder not to see me there.

AGAMEMNON
Good heaven!

IPHIGÉNIE
Mon père, vous vous taisez.

AGAMEMNON
Vous y serez, ma fille.

DUO
IPHIGÉNIE
Périsse le Troyen,
auteur de nos alarmes.

AGAMEMNON
Que de larmes sa perte
va coûter aux vainqueurs!

IPHIGÉNIE
Ah mon père, expliquez-vous.

AGAMEMNON
Je ne saurais t'en dire davantage.

IPHIGÉNIE
Dieux de la Grèce, veillez sur mon père.

AGAMEMNON
Dieux cruels, ne serez-vous point attendris?

TOUS DEUX ENSEMBLE
Périsse le Troyen,
auteur de nos alarmes.

SCÈNE III
IPHIGÉNIE
Quel trouble, ô Dieux, vient de jeter dans mon
coeur le froid accueil de mon père! Que dois-je
augurer de ces regards sombres, de ces mots
entrecoupés, de ces soupirs, de ces pleurs,
que ses yeux retenaient à peine!
Hélas, que cet accueil est différent de celui
que la douce espérance me promettait dans Argos!
Je verrai, disais-je en moi-même, mon père rempli
de joie venir au devant de nous, recevoir mes
embrassements, me tendre les bras.
À ses côtés seront Ménélas, Diomède, Ajax,
Achille, le fils de la Déesse, le plus vaillant des
Grecs, qui .....
hélas! mon père me fuit, personne ne paraît,
tout est dans l'abbattement, et dans la tristesse .....
Ô Déesse, qu'on révère dans cette contrée,
si votre culte m'a été cher,
si mes sacrifices ont été purs .....

SCÈNE IV
IPHIGÉNIE, CLYTEMNESTRE

CLYTEMNESTRE
Ah ma fille, sous quel astre malheureux
sommes-nous parties d'Argos! Quel accueil

IPHIGENIA
You speak not, sir!

AGAMEMNON
Child, you'll be there.

DUETTO
IPHIGENIA
Perish the Trojan, cause of all our grief.

AGAMEMNON
Conquest to pain like mine brings no relief.

IPHIGENIA
Why not explain to me this hidden woe?

AGAMEMNON
For your loved sake I cannot more relate.

IPHIGENIA
Ye guardian powers of Greece! protect my sire.

AGAMEMNON
Now, cruel Gods, relent in her behalf.

[both together]
Perish the Trojan cause of all our grief.

SCENE III
IPHIGENIA (*alone*)
This cold reception of a father chills me.
What can I gather from those lowering looks,
Those half formed words, deep sighs,
and starting tears!
[which his eyes could scarcely hold back.]
Alas! how different from what I hoped
Has our cold meeting been! Leaving Argos,
I fancied I should see my father haste
To joyfully embrace us as we came;
And with him as the attendants on his greatness
Ajax and Diomed and Menelaus
And Thetis' son, the bravest of them all,
Achilles, my betrothed, - by all neglected
I'm left alone; my father even shuns me.
What can have caused such consternation?
Say, virgin goddess, in this clime revered,
If e'er displeasing hath my worship proved,
Or if impure the sacrifice I made .....

SCENE IV
IPHIGENIA, CLYTEMNESTRA

CLYTEMNESTRA
Ah daughter under what unhappy star
Came we from Argos to ill-boding Aulis?

votre père et mon époux nous a-t-il fait!

IPHIGÉNIE
Les soins de l'état et de la guerre
l'absorbent maintenant
et le font paraître moins sensible
et moins tendre.

CLYTEMNESTRE
Non, non: il y a quelque autre cause que je saurai
pénétrer: Je saurai tout d'Arcas,
de cet esclave fidèle
que m'a donné Tindare mon père, et qui a suivi
Agamemnon à l'armée. Qu'il tarde de s'offrir à mes
yeux! Mais, ma fille, quels soins si pressants
peuvent donc retenir Achille?
C'est à son nom qu'Agamemnon nous a fait venir
en Aulide. Quels ennemis a-t-il maintenant à
combattre? La mer nous sépare de Troye, des fils
de Priam et du vaillant Hector. Ne vous a-t-il pas
demandé comme le prix du sang qu'il doit verser
aux bords de Xanthe? Que ne vient-il recevoir
ce prix qu'il a tant souhaité?

IPHIGÉNIE
Hélas, de quels nouveaux malheurs les Dieux
menaçent-ils la race de Tantale.

AIR
CLYTEMNESTRE
Quoique femme au milieu d'une armée,
je saurai bien me venger
et d'Agamemnon et d'Achille.
Celui qui aura offensé ma dignité
ne pourra jamais se vanter
d'être impuni.

IPHIGÉNIE
Dieux, serait-ce Achille lui-même? on l'accusait à
tort.

SCÈNE V
IPHIGÉNIE, CLYTEMNESTRE, ACHILLE
(*Achille est suivi d'une Troupe de Soldats couronnés
de laurier, de Captives Lesbiennes et d'Esclaves, qui
portent des trophées, des vases, des trépieds et
d'autres dépouilles de l'ennemi.*)

ACHILLE
Princesse, le bonheur d'Achille
est entre vos mains.
Puisse-je bientôt faire voir par les exploits que les
Dieux ont promis à mon bras, qu'Achille n'était
pas indigne des voeux de la fille d'Agamemnon.
Et vous, Madame, Thétis ne saurait que s'applaudir
que j'associe à une Déesse
la femme du Roi des Rois.

With what indifference has the king received us!

IPHIGENIA
The cares of state weigh heavy on his mind,
His anxious thoughts to carry on the war
For crushing Troy usurp his whole regard;
And for awhile make tenderness subside.

CLYTEMNESTRA
No; - 'tis some other cause, to me unknown,
But which ere long I'll learn; I'll draw't from Arcas:

That faithful slave by Tindarus, my father,
To me was given, whom I to Agamemnon
Have resigned -- But what delays Achilles?

Invited in his name, we're hither come.
No intervening conquest can detain him.
From Hector, Priam, and from Troy's proud walls
We're by the sea divided – the prince asks
Your hand in marriage as a just reward
Of all the Trojan warriors he shall slay;
And yet he comes not – it is wond'rous all.

IPHIGENIA
Our hapless race is doomed to new disasters.

AIR
CLYTEMNESTRA
Though hemmed in by troops, and a woman, I'll [know
Nor sovereign, nor prince shall unpunished remain,
To efface an affront by a most vengeful blow.
If to our high station they offer a stain.

IPHIGENIA
Here comes Achilles – wrongly he's accused.

SCENE V
IPHIGENIA, CLYTEMNESTRA, ACHILLES
(*Achilles is followed by soldiers crowned with laurel;
Lesbian slaves, of both sexes, carrying trophies,
vases, and other spoils taken from the enemy.*)

ACHILLES
Hail, princess! Agamemnon's beauteous child;
On thee alone my happiness depends.
And may the exploits which I am doomed to achieve
Against Troy's chiefs insure me all your love.
    (*turns to Clytemnestra*)
Nor will my mother Thetis, though divine,
Blush Clytemnestra's sister to be called,
The queen and consort to the king of kings.

CLYTEMNESTRE
Seigneur, puisse ce jour être aussi heureux, qu'il est doux à mon coeur! Et puisse ma fille faire revivre Achille dans votre posterité!

IPHIGÉNIE
Quelque sort que les Dieux me préparent,
Iphigénie sera trop heureuse d'avoir eu place à côté
de la Gloire dans le coeur d'Achille.

ACHILLE
Souffrez que je vous présente dans ces dépouilles
de Lesbos les premiers tributs de ma valeur:
Et vous, (*aux Captifs*)
apprenez à connaître votre Maîtresse et la mienne.

CHOEUR DES CAPTIVES
Le bras d'Achille a triomphé de Lesbos;
les yeux d'Iphigénie ont triomphé
de notre Vainqueur.
Célébrons à jamais
le pouvoir de l'Amour.

CHOEUR DES GRECS
L'heureux Achille va bientôt
sur son casque brillant
entrelasser les lauriers de Mars
avec les myrthes de l'Hymène.

UNE D'ENTRE LE CHOEUR DES CAPTIVES
O Simoïs, o Xanthe fleuves sacrés,
fleuves chéris des troupeaux
et des bergers,
des Dieux ennemis vont désoler
vos ravages,
vos eaux vont être ensanglantées
par la lance fatale
du belliqueux Achille.

UN D'ENTRE LE CHOEUR DES GRECS
Il vengera les Dieux de l'hospitalité,
que Pâris offença
dans la maison de ses Alliés.
Il vengera les maux,
que les sons effeminés
de la flûte Phrygienne
ont causés sur les bords de l'Eurotas.

TOUS
Le bras d'Achille a triomphé de Lesbos;
les yeux d'Iphigénie ont triomphé
du Vainqueur.
Célébrons à jamais
le pouvoir de l'Amour.

(*On danse.*)

CLYTEMNESTRA
Your words inspire me with the purest joy;
And may my daughter crown your love with heirs
That will rise equal to their father's fame.

IPHIGENIA
Whatever be the lot has prepared
For Iphigenia, 'tis her pride, her boast
To have rivalled glory in Achilles' heart.

ACHILLES
Deign to accept these spoils, obtained at Lesbos,
The first my valour has acquired. Captives,
(*to the Lesbians*)
Pay homage to your mistress and mine.

CHORUS of captives
Lesbos to bold Achilles yields,
    He sometimes will sweet thraldom prove;
His princess' arms preferred to shields.
    Be ever sung the power of love.

CHORUS of Greeks
This happy hero soon will twine
    With Mars' laurel Hymen's wreath
Around his helmet known to shine
    In the resistless scene of death.

One of the CHORUS of captives
How from their banks, the shepherd's joy,
Where flocks no more their care employ,
Will Xanthus and Simois' flood
Be by Achilles dyed in blood?
While adverse gods rage on the plain
And slaughter with her horrid train.

One of the CHORUS of Greeks
Thus the kind hospitable power
    Will just and ample vengeance take
On the vile swain of Ida's bower
    Who broke all laws for Helen's sake.

ALL TOGETHER
Lesbos to bold Achilles yields,
    He sometimes will sweet thraldom prove;
His princess' arms preferred to shields.
    Be ever sung the power of love.

A DANCE

ACTE III
Appartement de Palais.

SCÈNE I
AGAMEMNON
AIR

Douce Espérance, présent des Dieux,
   qui soulagez les mortels
   des maux qu'ils souffrent
par l'attente des biens qu'ils désirent:
Vous qui habitez avec tous les hommes,
   douce Espérance, ne m'abandonnez pas.

Les barbares qui aiment le carnage peuvent attribuer à la Divinité leur sauvage indignation. Mais je ne saurais pensé, que les Dieux soient capables d'un crime. J'entendrai bientôt moi-même leur voix. Assez et trop longtemps les Grecs ont été abusés par la voix des Devins. Sujets à se tromper, comme les autres mortels, la crédulité du vulgaire fait toute leur science. Mais hélas! d'où vient que je tremble d'interroger cet Oracle fatal? Si pourtant il demande ma fille, je ne saurais reculer sa mort un moment. Ah! voici Ulysse. Dieux! que je crains son approche!

SCÈNE II
AGAMEMNON & ULYSSE

ULYSSE
Venez, Seigneur, et reconnaissez ce nouveau gage de l'amitié d'Ulysse. Tout ce que j'avais prédit est arrivé en effet. Calchas a reçu votre demande avec indignation. Quoi? disait-il, la Religion est prophanée, nul respect pour les ordres des Dieux: Et l'on croit que ces Dieux nous seront favorables aux champs de Troye! Et c'est le Chef qui donne à la Grèce assemblée cet exemple d'irreligion!

AGAMEMNON
Il voudrait en effet ce Calchas être lui-même
le chef suprême de la Grèce,
commander l'armée et vingt Rois
par ses divinations et par ses prestiges.
Prophète sinistre
qui jamais n'a annoncé un bon augure,
ni fait la moindre chose digne de louange.

ULYSSE
Je crois, Seigneur, que j'aurais plutôt persuadé Pâris de rendre Hélène, que je n'aurais persuadé Calchas de vois introduire dans le Temple. Mais enfin les sentiments de père, les vertus d'Iphigénie, votre amour pour le bien public, votre soumission dès que vous aurez entendu les ordres du Ciel, les Dieux enfin m'ont dicté le discours que j'ai tenu à leur Pontife. J'ai appaisé sa colère: Il a consenti à ma demande et à la vôtre. Allons, Seigneur, tout est prêt. Les mêmes Dieux qui m'ont inspiré vous

ACT III
An apartment in the palace.

SCENE I
AGAMEMNON
AIR

Sweet hope, best gift of heaven to cheer
   Desponding mortals in their woe,
Or gild the gloomy shades of fear,
   And black despair to overthrow,
You raise the peasant to a throne;
   Do not my pious vow disown.

Let the fell monsters who delight in blood
Ascribe their savage nature to the gods.
I can't think heaven commands atrocious crimes;
Nay, I'm determined to consult its will,
No more imposed on by designing priests.
Too long the ear of Greece has been deceived
By such who're like ourselves to error prone.
A mob implicit raises them to power: -
And yet, why thus reluctant to proceed?
If the oracle demands my child – she dies.
Ulysses comes; I tremble lest he chide.

SCENE II
AGAMEMON, ULYSSES

ULYSSES
Now learn the friendly effort I have made
To win stern Calchas to approve your wish;
Who first indignant at my offer mild
Exclaimed, 'Is our religion scorned? By whom?
Our chief, who should the first example give
Of due obedience to the gods' decree;
Else must we never hope to conquer Troy.'

AGAMEMNON
Imperious, haughty priest, whose towering pride
Would fain usurp supreme authority;
And lord it over all the kings of Greece
By his false prophecies and juggling dreams.
His tongue, ill-omened to Atreus' house,
Ne'er yet aught pleasing to our ears foretold;
Nor hath he done a deed good men would praise.

ULYSSES
I thought, as soon I should from Paris gain
Helen to be returned to Menelaus
As your admission to the sacred temple.
But I such powerful arguments have urged
For sire, for daughter, for your patriot cares,
And homage to the gods (their will made known)
That forced him to relent – let's hither now,
And the same gods who fired me in your cause
Will to yourself declare the award of heaven.

admettent à leur présence.

SCÈNE III CLYTEMNESTRE, IPHIGÉNIE ET LES MÊMES	SCENE III CLYTEMNESTRA, IPHIGENIA, AGAMEMNON, ULYSSES

CLYTEMNESTRE
Arrêtez, Seigneur, il faut éclaircir un mystère.

CLYTEMNESTRA
Stop, sir, unfold what mystery contrived.

AGAMEMNON
Ah, Madame, laissez-moi aller où m'appellent
les destinées de ma famille et de la Grèce.

AGAMEMNON
'Tis now no time to ask: I must be gone
To learn what destiny the gods intend us.

SCÈNE IV CLYTEMNESTRE & IPHIGÉNIE	SCENE IV CLYTEMNESTRA, IPHIGENIA

CLYTEMNESTRE
Ah, ma fille! Il se dérobe à notre vue. Il va hâter
sans doute les cruelles destinées de sa famille. Je
ne m'étonne plus qu'interdit dans ses discours,
il ait paru nous revoir à regret.

CLYTEMNESTRA
Alas, my child! your father flies our sight,
He's gone to hasten some disastrous act:
Hence, faltering words, and so much grief.

IPHIGÉNIE
Hélas!

IPHIGENIA
Ah me!

CLYTEMNESTRE
Vous ne savez pas vos malheurs, ma fille.

CLYTEMNESTRA
You know not all your sorrows yet.

IPHIGÉNIE
Que dites-vous, Madame?

IPHIGENIA
What means the queen?

CLYTEMNESTRE
Arcas vient de me rendre
en ce moment une lettre,
qu'il avait ordre de me rendre en chemin.

CLYTEMNESTRA
This note by Arcas, given
But now into my hand, imparts the king
Had sent us orders to return to Argos.

IPHIGÉNIE
Eh bien, Arcas ne venait-il pas presser notre arrivée?

IPHIGENIA
How! not to hasten our arrival here?

CLYTEMNESTRE
Votre père m'ordonnait de reprendre la route
d'Argos sous prétexte qu'Achille voulait différer
son hymen; mais en effet pour s'ouvrir, dit-on, le
chemin de Troye votre père devait vous immoler.

CLYTEMNESTRA
And the pretext was that Achilles' will
Was to defer his nuptials till fallen Troy
Should yield to you its conqueror renowned.
Alas! the purport was to sacrifice thee.

IPHIGÉNIE
Dieux!

IPHIGENIA
Good heaven! –

CLYTEMNESTRE
Arcas s'est égaré en chemin.

CLYTEMNESTRA
Arcas mistook his way – Ruin!

IPHIGÉNIE
Vous ne m'auriez donné le jour, et ne m'auriez
élevée que pour être immolée aux Grecs et
immolée par un père. Les cruels! Ils me
conduisent au milieu d'Aulide sur un char de
triomphe, ils allumaient les flambeaux de l'Hymen.
Hymen fatal! on me destinait au fils de la Déesse,

IPHIGENIA
Have I been born for such an hapless end?
In public sacrificed before the Greeks!
Cruel deceivers! how they lured my hopes
On a triumphal car through Aulis' streets,
To light the torches for the rites of Hymen.
I was intended for Achilles' bride,

et je suis livrée à la mort.

CLYTEMNESTRE
Non, ma fille, vous ne le serez pas.
Je saurai vous défendre de la cruauté d'un père.
Achille comment pourrait-il souffrir, sans
commettre son honneur, qu'on abusât de son
nom? Quoi? ce serait lui-même
qui vous conduirait à l'autel!

(Elle veut sortir)

IPHIGÉNIE
Ah non, arrêtez, Madame. Mon père,
qui voulait nous faire retourner à Argos, saura
peut-être se sauver au milieu même de l'armée;
lui qui y tient le rang suprême,
et qui a toujours aimé Iphigénie.
Mais, hélas, de quels yeux reverrai-je Argos?
Moi qui en étais partie
au milieu des concerts, des danses,
pour être l'épouse d'Achille; moi qui est fille
d'Agamemnon et de Clyemnestre, fille de Thétis,
devais régner à Pthie dans les riches
maisons de Pélée,
et qui dans la race d'Achille étais destinée
à donner de nouveaux Héros à la Grèce.
Non, laissez-moi mourir. Je mourrai au moins
remplissant sans murmure la destinée
à laquelle m'appellent les ordres d'un père, et les
Dieux. Je mourrai sans déshonneur.

CLYTEMNESTRE
Hélène soeur fatale à la maison des Atrides,
qui troublez toute la Grèce, qui mettez en armes
l'Europe contre l'Asie, qui vous me coûtez de
larmes! Ce n'était pas assez que vous eussiez
déshonoré la couche de Ménélas. Faudrât-il
encore qu'Agamemnon se souille du sang
d'Iphigénie avant de vous ravir d'entre les bras
de votre indigne Phrygien?

IPHIGÉNIE
Ah, Madame, que je prévois de malheurs,
si vous n'êtes soumise aux ordres d'Agamemnon,
et si vous voulez me dérober à la mort. Vous voilà
désobéissante à votre époux: lui-même désobéirait
aux Dieux, sans l'ordre desquels
sans doute il ne me sacrifierait pas.
Si Achille
prend ma défense,
la Discorde s'empare des chefs de l'armée;
tout ordre est renversé. Les Dieux seuls
connaissent ce qui pourrait en arriver.

Now I'm devoted to untimely death.

CLYTMNESTRA
It shall not be, your mother will oppose
And snatch you from the assassinating hands
Of parent. – Brave Achilles, cruel too,
Shall join in my resentment to chastise
A plot thus varnished in that prince's name.
It makes him sharer in the monstrous crime;
A crime which he'll not easily forgive.

(about to leave)

IPHIGENIA
Ah1 be not so incensed against my sire,
The letter proves he meant to save my life
By his commanding our return to Argos.
Perhaps he may some expedient find
To save me from impending destiny:
He's here all-powerful and he loves his daughter,
But with what eyes can I revisit Argos?
I who thence parted 'midst acclaiming crowds,
'Midst festive music and a dance of joy;
I that was going to espouse Achilles,
To be acknowledged queen of Pthia's realm;
That there made happy in Achilles' love,
I should a race of heroes give to Greece
Who would not prove unworthy of their sire.
But such vain thoughts adieu – now welcome fate!
I will resign: and without murmuring die,
Since so my father and the gods resolve,
Nor shall there be a cause to blame my conduct.

CLYTEMNESTRA
Helen, how fatal to the race of Atreus!
Shame of thy sex and a reproach to Greece,
Thy baneful beauty proves thus kindling war
Between the powers of Europe and Asia. -
What tears you make me shed! Was't not enough
To have dishonoured the chaste nuptial bed
Of Menelaus, but a brother's child
Must for your wantonness be sacrificed?

IPHIGENIA
Unless you can command your sorrow more,
I well foresee more mischiefs will ensue;
Should you attempt to interpose 'twere vain:
Such disobedience to a husband's will,
E'en could you gain on him, would nought avail,
Because he'd too rebel against the gods:
But if Achilles' sword should interfere
To rescue Iphigenia from such woe,
Discord among the Grecian chiefs would rage,
Order must fly this camp, and heaven alone
Can tell how such a mutiny would end.

AIR

Que je meure obéissante
aux ordres des Dieux,
que j'achève une vie
qui m'exposerait peut-être
à des malheurs pires
encore que la mort même:
Que je sauve par ma mort
les maux qui menaçent
ma famille et la Grèce;
qui menaçent Achille.

SCÈNE V
CLYTEMNESTRE

Se pourrait-il qu'Agamemnon voulut immoler une fille si vertueuse! Ambition, Tyran des Rois, que ne peux-tu sur le coeur des mortels orgueilleux? Les Dieux se plairaient-ils à commander des crimes?

AIR

Allons nous éclaircir,
allons déchirer le voile importun,
qui couvre encore mes yeux:
Nous verrons après le parti
qu'il saura prendre.

SCÈNE VI
(*Le Théâtre représente l'intérieur du Temple de Diane.*)
AGAMEMNON, ULYSSE, CALCHAS, CHOEUR DES PRÊTRES

CHOEUR DES PRÊTRES
En vain les mortels tentent
de se soustraire aux ordres des Dieux.

UN DU CHOEUR
Les ordres des Dieux sont gravés
sur l'airain de l'Éternité.

DEUX DU CHOEUR
Le temps ne saurait le consumer;
ni la force, ni l'adresse des hommes
ne sauraient le briser.

(*Une partie des Prêtres danse gravement autour de l'autel de la Déesse.*)

UN DU CHOEUR
Les Rois sont sujets
aux décrets des Dieux,
ainsi que les Bergers.

TOUT LE CHOEUR
Jupiter incline sa tête immortelle:
l'Olympe tremble;
et l'Univers se tait.

AIR

Now let me end the cares of life,
Nor be exposed to longer strife;
But let my death prevent the woe
That ready seems on Greece to flow.

SCENE V
CLYTEMNESTRA

So good, so mild, so excellent a child
Can heaven command a father to destroy?
No – fell ambition, nature's surest foe,
That prompts, and not the gods, to such a crime.

AIR

I cannot yet discern
That the decree is truth,
The whole I'll strive to learn
And thereby save her youth.

SCENE VI
(*The theatre represents the interior view of the temple of Diana.*)
AGAMEMNON, ULYSSES, CALCHAS, CHORUS OF PRIESTS

CHORUS OF PRIESTS
'Twere a vain proof of mortal pride
To think heaven's will to put aside.

One of the CHORUS
The orders which from gods emane
Engraved on adamant remain.

Two of the CHORUS
The eternal tables of their will
Neither by time nor human skill
Can shew the least impression made,
Nor years nor force can them invade.

(*A part of the priests dance solemnly around the altar of the goddess.*)

One of the CHORUS
They rule the events of night and day,
Shepherds and kings alike they sway.

All the CHORUS
Behold Jove gives the almighty nod,
Olympus trembles 'fore its god:
Our low world is to silence hushed,

Lest in his anger it be crushed.

CALCHAS
Approchez, Agamemnon, et regardez comme
faveur signalée de la Déesse, qu'on vous accorde
qu'elle soit interrogée une seconde fois.

CALCHAS
Through special favour, Agamemnon, learn
The goddess here adored a second time
Now deigns that you interrogate her shrine.

DEMI AIR
Et vous Déesse fille de Jupiter,
   qui vous plaisez
   dans la solitude des vallées
   et dans l'ombre des forêts,
   ne regardez dans la démarche
   d'Agamemnon
   que la piété d'un père.
Mais si mes voeux ont toujours été
   pour le bien de la Grèce,
   si mes sacrifices vous ont été chers;
Parlez, Déesse. redemandez
   votre victime, et vengez
   l'honneur de vos Ministres
   offensé par l'incrédulité.

HALF-AIR
Thou goddess, sprung from mighty Jove,
   Who pleasant hills, sweet vales below
   And bloomy wood delightest to rove,
   O pity a fond father's woe!

If all my prayers for Greece's good
   And duteous immolations made
You like – O! be not now withstood,
   But have your oracle obeyed.

Speak, goddess, claim your victim now, -
   While incredulity exists,
Who henceforth at your shrine will bow;
   Speak, goddess, speak, revenge your priests.

AGAMEMNON
Ah! si l'âge, si l'innocence, si la beauté,
si la piété envers les dieux, envers vous-même,
Déesse, que j'adore en ces lieux, et dont je
crains les oracles ...
(*Tandis qu'Agamemnon parle, on entend un bruit
comme du tonnerre fort éloigné qui augmente peu à
peu.*)

AGAMEMNON
O! let her beauty, innocence and youth,
Her piety to heaven and chief to you,
Chaste goddess, object of my worship too,
Plead strong in Iphigenia's behalf.
(*While Agamemnon speaks a noise as of thunder is
heard, gradually increasing.*)

CALCHAS
La Déesse va parler.

CALCHAS
Mortals attend; the goddess means to speak.

L'ORACLE DANS LE FOND DU THEÂTRE
'Grecs, si vous voulez aborder à Troye,
Répandez dans l'Aulide le sang d'Iphigénie.'

The ORACLE
If, Grecians, ye expect to land at Troy,
The blood of Iphigenia must be shed.

AGAMEMNON
Hélas!

AGAMEMNON
What cruel sounds to a fond father's ear.

LE CHOEUR
Les Rois sont sujets
   aux décrets des Dieux,
   ainsi que les Bergers.

CHORUS
High heaven's decrees ne'er know decay,
Shepherds and kings alike they sway.

DEUX DU CHOEUR
Mille vaisseaux cachaient les mers:
   les ravages et les collines
   étaient couvertes
   par les chariots de guerre.

Two of the CHORUS
Where now the thousand ships combined
   That shadowed all yon stretching shore;
   And warlike chariots, fleet as wind,
   That covered plains? they're seen no more.

UN DU CHOEUR
Où sont-ils maintenant?

[One of the CHORUS
Where are they now?]

TOUT LE CHOEUR
Ils ont été dispersés par le souffle
   des Dieux irrités
   par la désobéissance.

All the CHORUS
To punish the reluctant mind
   Of Agamemnon has loud fate
Excited a tempestuous wind,

CALCHAS
Allez, Seigneur, soumettez-vous
aux ordres des Dieux.

LE CHOEUR
Les ordres des Dieux sont gravés
sur l'airain de l'Éternité.

CALCHAS
Seigneur, songez que ce sacrifice va vous ouvrir le
champ de gloire,
qui vous attend sous les murs d'Ilion.
Voyez les vaisseaux Grecs couvrir l'Hélléspont, et
voler à Troye parmi les acclamations des matelots
et des soldats: voyez ces mêmes vaisseaux,
les poupes couronnés et chargés de dépouilles
fendre une seconde fois ces mêmes mers; voyez
la Grèce entière, qui vous appelle de loin, vous
reçoit du rivage et chante votre triomphe. Allez,
Seigneur, soumettez-vous aux ordres des Dieux.

AGAMEMNON
Hélas!

LE CHOEUR
Les ordres des Dieux sont gravés
sur l'airain de l'Éternité.
Les Roi y sont sujets,
ainsi que les Bergers.
Jupiter incline sa tête immortelle:
l'Olympe tremble;
et l'Univers se tait.

ACTE IV
Gallérie du Palais.

SCÈNE I
AGAMEMNON seul
(*Une courte symphonie pathétique doit faire
l'ouverture de la Scène.*)
Je l'ai donc entendu cet Oracle funeste!
'Grecs, si vous voulez aborder à Troye,
Répandez dans l'Aulide le sang d'Iphigénie.'
Il faut donc obéir aux ordres des Dieux!

SCÈNE II
AGAMEMNON, CLYTEMNESTRE, IPHIGÉNIE

CLYTEMNESTRE
Je vous retrouve enfin, Seigneur, et parmi les soins
de l'état et de l'armée
la voix de Clytemnestre peut se faire entendre.
On avait voulu nous faire croire
(sur quel fondement je l'ignore) qu'Achille

They're now all in a shattered state.

CALCHAS
Sir, be advised, provoke not by delay:
Obey the oracle lest ills ensue.

The CHORUS
The orders which from gods emane
Engraved on adamant remain.

CALCHAS
Who'll profit most by such a sacrifice?
Yourself; - opens it not your road to glory?
Victory beckons from the Trojan shore,
And bids you haste to reap a laurelled harvest.
The Hellespont again will gladly foam
Beneath your ships, cheered by the sailors' shouts!
Ere long will they return surcharged with spoils -
Think as you land in Greece how crowds on crowds
Will welcome your approach and sing your triumph.
These sure are motives to command respect
To that decree you've in the temple heard.

AGAMEMNON
My heart's so full words cannot find a way.

The CHORUS
The orders which from gods emane
Engraved on adamant remain.
High heaven's decrees n'er know decay,
Shepherds and kings alike they sway.
Behold, Jove gives the almighty nod,
Olympus trembles 'fore its god;
Our low world is to silence hushed,
Lest in his anger it be crushed.

ACT IV
A gallery in the palace.

SCENE I
AGAMEMNON, alone
(*The scene opens to pathetic music.*)
Too plain I heard the oracle's decree,
'Grecians, if you expect to land at Troy,
The blood of Iphigenia must be shed.'
[So I must obey the commands of the gods!]

SCENE II
AGAMEMNON, CLYTEMNESTRA, IPHIGENIA.

CLYTEMNESTRA
Now, sir, we're met, though midst the din of arms
And crowding cares of your supreme command
Let, sir, your queen's, a mother's voice be heard.
My child and I have been seduced from Argos,
Hither to haste that she might wed Achlles.

voulait différer son hymen avec Iphigénie
jusqu'à son retour de Troye, mais lui-même,
Seigneur, vient de presser cet hymen,
et ne veut partir de l'Aulide qu'à ce prix.

AGAMEMNON
Madame, c'est à moi de disposer de ma fille.

CLYTEMNESTRE
Cruel, il est inutile de dissimuler;
sachez que j'ai tout appris.

AGAMEMNON
Ah! malheureux Arcas, tu m'as trahi.

IPHIGÉNIE
Non, non, mon père, vous n'êtes point trahi. Dès
que vous ordonnerez, vous serez obéi. Ma vie est
votre bien; je saurai vous la rendre dès que vous la
demanderez. Je saurai offrir mon sein sur le fer de
Calchas et respecter le coup ordonné par
vous-même.
Si pourtant mon obéissance et mon respect
paraissent dignes d'une autre récompense,
j'ose dire que ma vie était environné d'assez
d'honneurs pour ne pas souhaiter de la perdre à la
fleur de mon âge. C'est moi qui la première vous
appellai du doux nom de père, et que vous
honnorâtes du nom de votre fille. C'est moi
qui, reçue la première dans vos bras, épuisai
par mille caresses la tendresse paternelle. C'est moi
que vous aviez destinée au fils de la Déesse,
à un Prince digne de votre alliance. Hélas! avec
quel plaisir ne me faisais-je compter les noms des
pays que vous alliez dompter ensemble. Je ne
m'attendais pas, pour commencer ce triomphe,
mon sang fut le premier qu'on dût verser.

AGAMEMNON
Ma fille, il n'est que trop vrai: J'ignore pour quel
crime la vengeance des Dieux demande une
victime telle que vous, mais ils vous ont nommé.
Les Grecs ne sauraient aborder à Troye que votrre
sang ne soit versé.
Calchas l'avait annoncé, et moi-même je viens
d'entendre cet Oracle funeste, qui a prononcé
contre vous pour la seconde fois. Que n'avais-je
peint fait pour vous sauver? Je vous avais sacrifié
l'intérêt de la Grèce, mon rang, ma sûreté.
Arcas allait vous défendre l'entrée du camp.
Les Dieux l'ont égaré en chemin.
Ne vous assurez pas sur ma puissance.
En vain je combattais contre ces Dieux cruels
et contre la fureur des Grecs.
Votre heure est arrivée;
ma fille, il faut céder. Mais en mourant
faites connaître l'injustice des Dieux
et le sang d'Agamemnon.

Then we are told the prince has changed his mind
Nor will in marriage join till Troy's o'erthrown;
Yet he in person urges the espousal
And will not hence depart on other terms.

AGAMEMNON
The right's in me to rule my daughter's fate.

CLYTEMNESTRA
I know it is, thou barbarous cruel father.
Why now dissemble? I have learned your plot.

AGAMEMNON
Then the false Arcas has betrayed my secret.

IPHIGENIA
No, royal sir, you have not been betrayed. -
When you'll command I'm ready to obey.
My life is yours; you'll take but what you have:
And you shall find I'll die a hero's daughter,
Nor will my bosom shrink from Calchas' knife.

However, if obedient innocence
And full submission to the will of heaven
Were worthy of a better fate, my lot
Is hard indeed from such inviting joys
To be thus prematurely torn, in life's
Gay bloom; - and, O sir! deign to remember
That the once loved but now lost Iphigenia
First called you by the tender name of father;
And in return you called her that of child.
Me you've long destined for Achilles' bride,
Because a hero worthy your alliance.
And with what joy used I to hear recounted
The various kingdoms ye were both to conquer.
I did not think the auspice of your triumphs
Was to be sought in Iphigenia's blood.

AGAMEMNON
'Tis but too true; nor can I yet conceive
By what crime I've deserved the ire of heaven,
But you are named, nor is't in mortal power
To elude its high behest:
                the murmuring Greeks,
By Calchas' tongue insatiate for your blood,
Will mutiny and execute by force
What better were submitted to with mildness.
Long did I force myself to doubt, but now
The oracle a second time has spoke. -
Unlucky Arcas was dispatched to meet you
And interdict your coming to the camp.
By that intent what dangers I provoked
Both to our rank and realm, to Greece combined,
But heaven thought otherwise and from the path
He should have taken made faithful Arcas stray.
Vain then on my side would prove all attempts.
The fatal hour is come; when dying shew
The oracle's unjust and you're my daughter.

CLYTEMNESTRE Vous ne me démentez pas votre race: Vous êtes le sang d'Atrée et de Thyeste: Bourreau de votre fille, il ne vous reste plus que d'en faire un festin à la mère. Ainsi donc je l'aurai amenée au supplice! Je m'en retournerai seule par les chemins parsemés encore des fleurs qu'on a jetés sur son passage! Je reverrai Argos …	**CLYTEMNESTRA** Thou dost not, monster, now bely thy race; Of the same blood with Atreus and Thyestes. Barbarian, canst thou thus condemn a child? – Next send her breathless corse for me to feast on? Have I then brought her hither to be butchered, And must I childless now return to Argos By the same roads where flowers were strewed before her?

AIR
Ah non, je ne souffrirai jamais
   qu'on arrache ma fille
   d'entre mes bras,
   ou vous serez aux Grecs
un seul sacrifice de la fille et de la mère.
	AIR
	Misled Greeks, touch not my child:
	   The rash attempt you'll surely rue.
	Vain on oracles you build,
	   With her kill her mother too.

SCÈNE III LES MÊMES ET ACHILLE	**SCENE III** ACHILLES, AGAMEMNON, CLYTEMNESTRA and IPHIGENIA
ACHILLE Seigneur, un bruit bien étrange est venu jusqu'à moi; mais je l'ai jugé peu digne de croyance. On dit, je ne puis le redire sans horreur, qu'Iphigénie aujourd'hui expire, qu'appellée sous mon nom en Aulide je ne la conduisais à l'autel que pour y être immolée. Que faut-il que j'en pense, Seigneur?	**ACHILLES** Sir, I'm alarmed at the report I've heard And scarce can think it true: that in thy name, From Argos hither Iphigenia called Is in the temple to be sacrificed. Have I then, sir, your instrument been made To lure the princess from her native home For an intent so horrid and 'gainst nature?
AGAMEMNON Je ne rends point compte de mes desseins. Quand il en sera temps, vous apprendrez le sort de ma fille et l'armée en sera instruite.	**AGAMEMNON** Those of my rank for what they please to do Are not accountable to inferiors. But when the proper moment is arrived You and all Greece shall learn my daughter's fate.
CLYTEMNESTRE Père cruel!	**CLYTEMNESTRA** Execrable tyrant!
ACHILLE Ah je ne sais que trop le sort que vous lui réservez.	**ACHILLES** Evasive king, Too well I know the fate which you intend.
AGAMEMNON Pourquoi, si vous le savez, le demandez-vous donc?	**AGAMEMNON** Why ask of me what you already know?
ACHILLE Ô Ciel, pourquoi je le demande? Osez-vous avouer le plus noir des crimes? Mais pensez-vous qu'Achille, oubliant sa foi et son honneur, laisse immoler Iphigénie?	**ACHILLES** Patience, ye gods! – Why ask? – Can your heart own So black, so impious a resolution. But if it does – then think not that Achilles Will be a tame spectator of thy crime. His love, his honour, urge him to protect her.
IPHIGÉNIE Hélas! le Ciel m'a rendue assez malheureuse sans que j'allume encore une colère fatale entre mon père et celui qu'on avait nommé mon époux. Laisse-moi mourir, Seigneur: J'apporte trop d'obstacles à votre gloire.	**IPHIGENIA** Good heaven, what mischief am I like to cause! Fatal dissension 'twixt my honoured sire And the loved hero I once hoped to wed. No, let me die and put an end to all The rising obstacles to certain glory:

Vous ne pouvez aborder à Troye qu'au prix de mon sang. Allez, faites pleurer ma mort aux veuves des Troyens. Si je n'ai pu vivre la compagne d'Achille, j'espère que votre nom et le mien seront joints ensemble à jamais et que ma mort sera la source de votre gloire.	Since 'tis decreed ye cannot land at Troy But through the effusion of my hapless blood. There let your valiant deeds make Trojan dames In their lost sons and husbands rue my fall. Though 'tis forbid that I shall be your bride, Yet will our names be joined through ages down And my death deemed the source of all your glory.
ACHILLE	ACHILLES
Non, vous ne mourrez pas. Tant que je vivrai, tant que ces yeux verront la lumière, je saurai, l'épée à la main, défendre mes droits contre qui que ce soit dans l'armée fut-il revêtu du rang suprême.	Talk not of dying while Achilles lives And that my eyes behold yon radiant sun. With this good executive sword of mine The foremost of them all shall bite the ground, Who'd arrogantly dare dispute my right.
AGAMEMNON	AGAMEMNON
Mais vous qui menaçez ici, oubliez-vous à qui vous parlez?	Such menaces, and in our presence too, Become thee not; nor will I suffer, prince.
ACHILLE	ACHILLES
Et vous, oubliez-vous que c'est Achille que vous outragez. Non, je vous le répète, votre fille ne mourra point: Cet Oracle est plus sûr que celui de Calchas.	Become me not! when Agamemnon dares To wrong me in the tenderest part, my love. If thou'rt a king o'er kings, know I'm Achilles And that I've sworn your daughter shall not die.
AGAMEMNON	AGAMEMNON
Grands Dieux! ne suis-je donc plus son père?	And will you, prince, dispute a father's power?
ACHILLE	ACHILLES
Non, elle n'est plus à vous. On ne m'abuse pas par de vaines paroles. N'est-ce pas pour moi que vous l'avez mandée d'Argos?	Your power of father is no more; she's mine By love, by promise mine; was't not to wed With Peleus' son that she from Argos came?
AGAMEMNON	AGAMEMNON
Plaignez-vous donc aux Dieux qui l'ont demandée: accusez Calchas, le camp tout entier, accusez Ménélas, Ulysse et vous tout le premier.	Implead the gods who've otherwise ordained; Blame the whole camp, Ulysses, Menelaus, Calchas, who're not so culpable as thou.
ACHILLE	ACHILLES
Moi?	I culpable?
AGAMEMNON	AGAMEMNON
Vous, qui quérellez à tous moments le Ciel qui nous arrête. Mon coeur vous avait ouvert une voie de la sauver; c'était de renoncer à notre entreprise; mais vous voulez courir à Troye: Allez-y, sa mort va vous en ouvrir le chemin.	Yes thou, whose wild ambition Was ever railing 'gainst the opposing gods That here detained us. I the means proposed By which she might be saved, but you rejected; And that was to decline the war with Troy; You'd hear of nought but Ilion overturned - Now thither haste, her blood insures its fall.
ACHILLE	ACHILLES
Barbare, perjure, et que m'a fait cette Troye? Jamais les vaisseaux de Scamandre osèrent-ils aborder aux champs de Thessalie? Jamais un ravisseur Phrygien vint-il enlever nos femmes? Si je cours à Troye, c'est pour laver votre honte. Faudra-t-il pour vous rendre Hélène, qu'on commence par me ravir Iphigénie?	Barbarian, - merciless and bloody king, What had Troy done to draw on my resentment? Thence no ships ever sailed for Thessaly, With hostile troops our subjects to invade; No Phrygian ravishers have ever dared To carry off their wives in haughty triumph. Is't not for you that I've 'gainst Priam leagued And fain would hasten his destruction, sir, That the foul stain of your illustrious line

Non, non, je ne connais ni Priam ni Pâris:
je veux votre fille et ne pars qu'à ce prix.
Allez, puissant Agamemnon,
nous verrons si sans Achille
vous oserez approcher de Troye.

QUATUOR
AGAMEMNON

Partez, fuyez,
assez d'autres sans vous
trouverons le chemin de l'Asie.
Je ne crains point votre courroux.

ACHILLE

Rendez grâces au Ciel,
qui vous a fait
le père d'Iphigénie -
Vous l'éprouveriez à l'heure même.

IPHIGÉNIE

Ah mon père, Achille, calmez votre colère,
Laissez-moi mourir.

CLYTEMNESTRE

Oracle barbare!
Père plus barbare encore!

TOUS

Dieux! quelle est donc
votre cruauté!

SCÈNE IV
CLYTEMNESTRE, IPHIGÉNIE

CLYTEMNESTRE

Le barbare fuit, et la livre à la mort.
Oh ma fille, oh mère infortunée!

IPHIGÉNIE

Ô Soleil, ô lumière éternelle,
Je ne verrai donc plus le flambeau du jour!
Il m'éclaire pour la dernière fois.

CLYTEMNESTRE

Achille combattra pour nous
et nous sauvera des mains d'un père dénaturé.

IPHIGÉNIE

Ah, ma mère, au nom des Dieux empêchez
qu'Achille ne prodigue pas sa vie pour sauver
la mienne. Que sort enfin de se flatter?
Diane veut sa victime.
Faible mortelle, puis-je résister à la Déesse?
soyons la victime de la Patrie. Vous vous taisez,
Madame, et vos yeux sont couverts de pleurs.

CLYTEMNESTRE

Infortunée que je suis,
n'ai je donc pas sujet de pleurer?

Might soon be washed away with Trojan blood?
For Helen's crime must your chaste daughter perish?
And she the only change for an adulteress!
Your daughter's mine, or I'll not move toward Troy;
Try then without me what your arms can do.

QUARTETTO
AGAMEMNON

Hence, part, begone, we want thee not,
Yet Troy shall tumble to the ground;
To live inglorious be thy lot,
'Mongst cowards will thy name be found.

ACHILLES

Thou faithless king, provoke me not,
Lest my sword fell thee to the ground;
To be her sire's thy happy lot,
Else 'mongst the slain thou now wert found.

IPHIGENIA

O prince! if me you ever loved,
Be not thus with anger moved.

CLYTEMNESTRA

Merciless fate, must she expire?
Oh! yet more merciless her sire!

ALL

By so barbarous a decree,
Immortal gods, how wretched we!

SCENE IV
CLYTMNESTRA, IPHIGENIA

CLYTEMNESTRA

Your father's gone and gives you up to fate.
O, my poor child, and are we thus to part!

IPHIGENIA

O, sun! thou cheering light to mortal eyes,
Soon Iphigenia will behold no more
Thy friendly beams. – I take my farewell view.

CLYTEMNESTRA

Do not despond, Achilles' love will save thee
And snatch thee from a tyrant father's power.

IPHIGENIA

O madam! in the name of all the gods
Persuade him not to risk his life for mine,
Of what avail to feed illusive hopes?
Diana is determined on her victim.
And to oppose her will would fruitless prove. -
No, for my country's good I die resigned. -
O, why thou silent, and why flow these tears?

CLYTEMNESTRA

Have I not cause to weep, my child? My tongue,
By grief opprest, denies its wonted use.

IPHIGÉNIE Ne m'attendrissez pas; songez plutôt à m'affermir.	**IPHIGENIA** Instead of adding to, support my weakness.
CLYTEMNESTRE Hélas! Je retournerai donc à Argos seule, sans ma fille. Arrivée à Argos, vainement dans ma triste solitude je demanderai Iphigénie aux lieux qu'elle habitait autrefois. Je la chercherai partout, et ne la reverrai jamais.	**CLYTEMNESTRA** Ah me! must I return alone to Argos Without my child; and when I'm there arrived In vain, to cheer my solitary walks, Shall I in fancy seek for Iphigenia.
IPHIGÉNIE Ah, ma mère, encore une fois, au nom des Dieux, ne m'attendrissez pas davantage; mais, Madame, accordez-moi une grâce.	**IPHIGENIA** Madam, once more have pity on your child, Nor with such tender plaints unnerve me. - There's one request I hope you'll not refuse.
CLYTEMNESTRE Parlez, je ne puis rien vous refuser.	**CLYTEMNESTRA** If in my power I can refuse thee nothing.
IPHIGÉNIE Que ni vos cheveux coupés ni vos voiles déchirées n'annoncent le regret de ma mort.	**IPHIGENIA** Then do not, on account of my disaster, Or by rent veil, torn or dishevelled locks Betray the least regret that I'm no more.
CLYTEMNESTRE Hélas! mais le retour à Argos que ferai-je pour vous?	**CLYTEMNESTRA** [Alas, how can I return to Argos without you?
IPHIGÉNIE Chérissez mon père et votre époux.	**IPHIGENIA** Look after my father and your husband.]
CLYTEMNESTRE Ah! il mérite d'essuyer les plus grands malheurs pour expier votre mort.	**CLYTEMNESTRA** Your death must draw down vengeance on his head.
IPHIGÉNIE C'est malgré lui et pour le bien de la Grèce qu'il m'a perdue.	**IPHIGENIA** My death's no crime of his; 'tis heaven's command; The welfare of the Greeks forced his assent.

CHOEUR DES FEMMES
Comme une fleur nouvelle
   coupée par la faux du moissonneur,
   telle sera la belle Iphigénie
   sous le couteau de Calchas.
	CHORUS of women
	As when cut down the lily fair
	   Declined, lies with fading charms,
	So with her bosom wounded, bare,
	   Will that bright nymph in death's cold arms.

DEUX D'ENTRE LE CHOEUR Dieux cruels, elle mourra!	**Two of the CHORUS** Ah! if so sweet a princess die, There's no compassion from on high.

IPHIGÉNIE
Non, je vivrai toujours
   comme l'heureuse libératrice
   de la Grèce.
	IPHIGENIA
	I shall be ever famed in story;
	The Greeks to me owe their glory.

UNE DU CHOEUR
Le flambeau de l'hymen
   devait vous éclairer;
   les ombres de la mort
   vont vous envelopper.
	One of the CHORUS
	Deserving of a longer date,
	She came to wed, but meets her fate.

CLYTEMNESTRE Dieux favorables,	**CLYTEMNESTRA** If any gods befriend our cause,

animez Achille,
donnez une force nouvelle
au bras de notre vengeur.
                (*Clytemnestre sort.*)
	Oh! rouse Achilles to take arms.
	Now the destuctive sword he draws
	And shields young Iphigenia's charms.
	                (*Exit.*)

UNE DU CHOEUR Princesse digne d'un meilleur sort, vous espériez trouver Achille à l'autel; et vous y trouverez la mort.	One of the CHORUS Deserving of a longer date, She came to wed, but meets her fate.
IPHIGÉNIE J'y trouverai une gloire éternelle.	IPHIGENIA I shall be ever famed in story; To me the Greeks will owe their glory.
LE CHOEUR Comme une fleur nouvelle coupée par la faux du moissonneur, telle sera la belle Iphigénie sous le couteau de Calchas.	CHORUS As when cut down the lily fair Declined, lies with fading charms, So with her bosom wounded, bare, Will that bright nymph in death's cold arms.

ACTE V

SCÈNE I

Tente d'Achille.
CLYTEMNESTRE & ACHILLE

ACT V

SCENE I.

The tent of Achilles.
CLYTEMNESTRA, ACHILLES

ACHILLE Que vois-je? Vous ici, Madame?	ACHILLES What urgent cause brings Clytemnestra hither?
CLYTEMNESTRE Je ne dois point rougir de venir embrasser vos genoux pour ma fille, pour votre épouse, qui vous est enlevée. Le danger presse.	CLYTEMNESTRA I blush not, prince, to throw me at your feet, And beg your help for Iphigenia's life, Your lately promised bride – to death condemned, Unless you snatch her from the pressing woe.
ACHILLE Connaissez-vous donc si peu Achille, et ne vous fiez pas à ma parole?	ACHILLES And is it thus you know Achilles' spirit That you can now my sacred promise doubt?
CLYTEMNESTRE On apprête déjà le sacrifice impie, Seigneur.	CLYTEMNESTRA The horrid sacrifice they now prepare.
ACHILLE Ne perdons pas le temps en discours superflus. Allez, Madame, Achille sauvera votre fille.	ACHILLES Let's waste no time in words superfluous. [Go, Madam, Achilles will save your daughter.]
AIR J'en atteste mon amour, et vous en réponds sur mon épée: Elle sera abbreuvée du sang Grec avant de se tremper dans le sang Troyen.	*AIR* By my chaste love and thirst of fame This sword shall reek with Grecian blood. For ever die Achilles' name, If in her cause I be withstood.

SCÈNE II

(*Le Théâtre représente d'un côté le Bois et le Temple de Diane; de l'autre côté on voit une partie du camp des Grecs, le port de l'Aulide et la flotte.*

SCENE II.

(*The theatre represents on one side a wood and the temple of Diana; on the opposite side is seen a part of the Grecian camp, the port of Aulis and the fleet.*

Iphigénie, Agamemnon, Calchas, Ulysse, Arcas, puis Clytemnestre, Troupe de Prêtres, de Filles consacrées à Diane et de Soldats. [La Troupe s'avance du fond du Théâtre accompagnée d'une musique lugubre.])

CALCHAS
Déesse, qui prêtez à la nuit
 l'éclat du jour,
vous qui veillez du haut
 de l'Olympe au salut de la Grèce,
nous respectons vos ordres,
nous nous soumettons à vos oracles;
prenez votre victime, Déesse,
 et déchaînez les vents.

LE CHOEUR
Prenez votre victime, Déesse,
 et déchaînez les vents.

PARTIE DU CHOEUR
Pâris avec sa proye
 insulte de ses tours
à nos mille vaisseaux,
 qui la menaçent en vain.

CHOEUR
Prenez votre victime, Déesse,
 et déchaînez les vents.

IPHIGÉNIE
Me voici prête, ô mon père: Je me dévoue volontiers pour votre gloire, et pour la Grèce. Grecs, vous serez heureux, si votre bonheur ne dépend pas de ma mort. Que personne ne porte ses mains sur moi: Je présenterai mon sein: Conduisez moi comme une victime volontaire, victorieuse d'Ilion et fatale aux Phrygiens.

AGAMEMNON
Hélas!
      (Il se voile la tête.)

PARTIE DU CHOEUR
Tant de beauté et de vertu
 ne méritait pas un sort si cruel.

AUTRE PARTIE
Descendons sur le rivage de l'Ilion;
et que les Dieux de l'Ilion
 combattent contre nous.

LE CHOEUR
Prenez votre victime, Déesse,
 et déchaînez les vents.

CALCHAS
Grecs, écoutez-moi et formez d'heureux présages.

Iphigenia, Agamemnon, Calchas, Ulysses, Arcas first appear; then Clytemnestra, priests, virgins consecrated to Diana and attendant soldiers. They all advance from the bottom of the theatre to melancholy music.)

CALCHAS
Goddess, who gild the solemn night,
 While from thy orb mild beams do flow,
May Greece find favour in thy sight,
 Let loose the winds and bid them blow.

CHORUS
The victim take our vows do owe;
Let loose the winds and bid them blow.

Part of the CHORUS
Now Trojans with the guilty pair
 Mock at our fleet from their high towers,
But soon shall yield to black despair,
 All crushed by Grecian powers.

The CHORUS
Goddess, the victim take we owe;
Let loose the winds and bid them blow.

IPHIGENIA [*to Agamemnon*]
I'm ready, sir, and shall without a groan
My life resign, your glory to insure,
And make Greece triumph o'er the perjured foe.
Let none dare offer to lay hands on me;
I'll to the knife unmoved, my bosom bare.
I mean to die a voluntary victim,
In death triumphant and the bane of Troy.

AGAMEMNON
Alas, my child! my eyes can ne'er behold.
    (throws his cloak around his head.)

Part of the CHORUS
Such beauty, such undaunted spirit,
Should a more happy fortune merit.

Another part of the CHORUS
Soon shall we land on Ilion's shore
In spite of gods whom they adore.

THE CHORUS
Goddess, the victim take we owe,
Let loose the winds and bid them blow.

CALCHAS
Attend, ye Greeks, hence hope a lucky omen.

CLYTEMNESTRE
Dieux! Achille n'arrive point et Calchas va frapper.
(à part.)

(Calchas tire le glaive, le met dans un vase d'or, couronne la victime, prend une coupe d'eau sacrée, et s'avance vers l'autel.)

CALCHAS
Déesse, fille de Jupiter,
acceptez le sang d'Iphigénie,
et accordez-nous la prise de Pergame.

(Dans le moment qu'il va frapper on entend un bruit d'armes. Tout le monde tourne de ce côté là. Calchas continue:)

CALCHAS
Quel téméraire ennemi des Dieux
ose troubler le sacrifice?

SCÈNE DERNIÈRE
LES MÊMES, ACHILLE & DIANE EN L'AIR

ACHILLE
C'est Achille, qui défend ses droits.

DIANE
Achille, arrêtez, gardez votre courage
et cette soif de sang contre les Troyens.
Puisse le Père des Dieux empêcher toujours
que la colère n'anime Achille contre les Grecs
et ne retarde la chute d'Ilion.
Pour Iphigénie, elle est à moi.

(Elle s'envole. On voit une biche palpitante et toute ensanglantée à la place d'Iphigénie. Achille lève les mains au Ciel.)

CALCHAS
Ah prodige!

LE CHOEUR
Ah prodige!

CALCHAS
Le sang d'Iphigénie a paru trop précieux à la
Déesse pour le répandre sur ses autels.
C'en est fait, Agamemnon, Ulysse, Achille, Grecs,
la Déesse exauce nos voeux;
elle facilite notre course
et nous ouvre le chemin de Troye.

(On entend le sifflement des vents et le bruit de la mer, et voit remuer les vaisseaux.)

CLYTEMNESTRA
Achilles not yet come and Calchas' knife
Is ready drawn 'gainst Iphigenia's breast.   *(aside.)*

(Calchas, having put his drawn knife in a golden vase, crowns the victim; and with a cup of consecrated water in his hand advances towards the altar.)

CALCHAS
Thou goddess, daughter of immortal Jove,
Deign to accept young Iphigenia's blood.
For shedding it be Pergamus our prey.

[The moment he is going to strike a clash of arms is heard, towards which all turn.]

CALCHAS continuing
What sacrilegious mortals hither come
And interrupt our sacrifice to heaven?

The Last SCENE
Enter ACHILLES. DIANA at the same time is seen
in the air.

ACHILLES
Behold Achilles, who demands his right.

DIANA
Suspend your ire, O valiant son of Thetis!
And turn it tenfold 'gainst perfidious Troy.
May the great fire of all celestial powers
Forbid Achilles' wrath against the Greeks
Should rage and so prevent the fall of Troy.
Now Iphigenia as my prize I claim.

(Diana disappears, and in the room of Iphigenia is seen a doe panting and bloody; Achilles raises his hands to heaven.)

CALCHAS
A miracle!

LE CHOEUR
A miracle indeed!

CALCHAS
The princess' blood appeared of too much worth
To be effused in this our cause. The goddess
Takes her to herself, and henceforth to us
Indulgent she will favour all our wishes.
Ye Grecian warriors, now for Troy prepare
Your hostile arms; the obstacle's removed.

(The noise of a rising wind is heard, the sea thrown into agitation and the ships are all in motion.)

CHOEUR DES MATELOTS qui sont sur les vaisseaux, et que l'on entend de loin La mer s'agite, les flots s'élèvent, - les vents nous appellent.	A CHORUS of sailors in the ships is heard from a distance The sea is roused, the billows rise, The winds invite and Troy's our prize.
CHOEUR DES SOLDATS sur le devant du Théâtre qui répond Les vents nous appellent.	CHORUS OF SOLDIERS on the fore part of the Theatre The winds invite and Troy's our prize.
(Après que les deux Choeurs ont répondu alternativement à plusieurs reprises:)	*(After the two choruses, several times alternately sung, then:-)*
TOUT LE CHOEUR Pâris ne jouira longtemps de sa perfidie, les vents nous appellent, Troye est renversée, et la Grèce est vengée.	The full CHORUS of both Paris shan't long his crime enjoy; The winds invite; now, now we steer To punish him and conquer Troy. To injured Greece revenge is dear.
DANSE DE MATELOTS	A DANCE of sailors
FIN	END OF THE OPERA

A short Glossary of certain terms used in this work

Adagio, a slow tune.

Affetto, affettuoso, means that kind of music which is tender and moving.

Allegro, a brisk, lively, gay and pleasant style of music.

Aria, a song, air or tune.

Andamento, andante, andantissimo, these are derived from the Italian word *andare,* to go, and signify that the notes (especially in the thorough basses) are to be played distinctly and slow, from a less to the greatest degree.

Ballet, is of French origin and signifies a succession of airs in all sorts of movements, whether brisk or slow, with which the dances agree and are carried on as the strains or motions differ.

Bravura, is applied to whatever performance, instrumental or vocal, requires a spirited, lively and impassioned execution.

Cadenza. Cadence in modern music is a certain conclusion of a song or of the piece, which is divided as it were into so many numbers or periods. The cadence is when the parts fall, or terminate on a chord or note, the ear seeming naturally to expect it, and is much the same in a song as a period that closes the sense in a paragraph of discourse.[152]

---

[152] *Cadenza* is also used to mean an often florid improvised conclusion to a solo vocal or instrumental part, especially in an operatic aria - exactly the sort of thing that reform opera preferred to abjure.

Cantabile, cantilena, signify the first a piece of melody well composed, and the second a song.

Continuata, in vocal music means to continue or hold on a sound with an equal strength or manner, or to continue a movement in an equal degree of time all the way.

Descant, is to run a division or variety upon one, two or more given notes with an instrument or voice.

Diastematic, implies, according to the sense of the ancients, a simple interval in opposition to a compound one, by them called a system.

Finale, is the end or last note of a piece of music; but it more particularly means the close or last note of a tone or mode by which it is distinguished from all others; sometimes the end of airs.

Harmony, is the agreeable effect of sounds, differing in acuteness, produced together.

Melody, is the effect of sounds ranged and disposed in succession: so that melody is the effect of a single voice or instrument: which distinguishes it from harmony, though they are often confounded.

Obligato, signifies *for,* on purpose *for,* or necessary, as *duoi violini,* on purpose *for* two violins, and so of other instruments.

Orchestra, is that part of a theatre where the musicians are placed.

Phonic, comes from the Greek word φωνή, signifying voice or sound, and implies the doctrine or science of sound, called likewise *acoustics.*

Piano, soft or sweet, or gently slow.

Presto, quick or fast; and gaily, without being rapid.

Ripieno, signifies full; and is used in pieces of music in parts, to distinguish those parts that are played but now and then from what fill up those that are played throughout the piece.

Ritornello, the burden, or the repetition of the verses of a song at the end of each stanza. It means also those symphonies played before the voices begin by way of an introduction or prelude.

Svegliato, a gay, brisk, lively manner of playing or singing.

Symphony, signifies in music a concert or consonance of several sounds agreeable to the art, be they instrumental or vocal or both, and may be called harmony in general; yet some there are who confine the meaning of symphony to instrumental music alone and therefore say that the *symphonies* of such an opera were excellent, although the recitatives were abominable.

Violetta, this term signifies the *triple viol.*[153]

Virtù, signifies a superiority of genius and talents; and by *virtuoso* is meant a person thus eminently endowed by nature and due cultivation; wherefore an excellent painter, able architect etc. are called *virtuosi.* But this denomination seems to be appropriated by the Italians in a more especial manner to eminent musicians, and among them rather to those who apply themselves to the theory than to the practice of that art. The term *virtuoso* is understood in a very different sense by the English.[154]

F I N I S.

---

[153] I.e. the treble viol, precursor of the violin.
[154] In 18th century English the term *virtuoso* meant a scholar or connoisseur of the arts.

Bibliography

The bibliography lists in A the works quoted or referred to by Algarotti himself in the *Essay on the Opera*, showing something of the range of his reading, and in B modern works of which the editor has made use.

A. <u>Works cited by Algarotti</u>

ADDISON, Joseph, *The Spectator*, Vol. 1 No. 2, 6 March 1711.

ARISTOTLE, *Poetics*.

AVISON, Charles, *An Essay on Musical Expression*, 1752.

D'ALEMBERT, Jean, Preface (*Discours préliminaire*) to the *Encyclopaedia*, 1751.
-----, *Mélanges de littérature, de l'histoire et de philosophie*, 1759.

DANTE, *Inferno*.

DRYDEN, John, *Lines written to Sir Godfrey Kneller*, 1694.

HORACE, *Epistles*.

NORDEN, Frederick Ludvig, *Travels into Egypt*, 1755.

PERI, Jacopo, Preface to *Euridice*, 1601.

'PHILONUS,' *The World*, No. 156.

POPE, Alexander, *Epistle to the Earl of Burlington*, 1731.

SAINT-ÉVREMOND, Charles de, *Works* Vol. 3.

VITRUVIUS, *Eight Books on Architecture*.

VOLTAIRE, *Le mondain*, 1736.

WALLIS, John, *Strange effects reported of music in former times* (*Philosophical Transactions* abridged by John Lowthorp, Vol. 1),

WEBB, Daniel, *Remarks on the beauties of Poetry*, 1762.

XENOPHON, *In Hieronem.*

B. <u>Works cited in editorial matter</u>

ALGAROTTI, Francesco, *Saggio sopra l'opera in musica: Le edizioni del 1755 e del 1763,* ed. Annalisa Bini *(Libreria Editrice Musicale Italiana),* Rome 1989.

-----, *Essai sur l'opéra en musique (Saggio sopra l'opera in musica* in the revised 1764 version) (with Benedetto Marcello, *Le théâtre à la mode (Il teatro alla moda)* and other writings by Angiolini, Calzabigi, Metastasio and Du Roullet), ed. and tr. Jean-Philippe Navarre *(A.M.I.C.U.S., Les Éditions du Cerf),* Paris 1998.

BENEDETTI, Jean, *David Garrick and the Birth of Modern Theatre,* London 2001.

COOPER, Martin, *Gluck,* London 1935.

DENT, Edward J., *The Rise of Romantic Opera,* ed. Winton Dean, Cambridge 1976.

DORSCH, T. S., *Classical Literary Criticism: Aristotle, Horace, Longinus,* London 1965.

DRUMMOND, John D., *Opera in Perspective,* London 1980.

DRYDEN, John, *The Poems,* ed. John Kinsley, Oxford 1958.

FARA, Patricia, *Newton: the Making of Genius,* London 2003.

HEARTZ, Daniel, *From Garrick to Gluck: the Reform of Theatre and Opera in the Mid-18th Century,* Proceedings of the Royal Musical Association, London, Vol. XCIV (1967-68), pp.111-127

HERIOT, Angus, *The Castrati in Opera,* London 1956.

HOWARD, Patricia, *Gluck and the Rise of Modern Opera,* London 1963.
-----, *C. W. von Gluck, Orfeo* (Cambridge Opera Handbooks), Cambridge 1981.
-----, *Gluck: an 18th Century Portrait in Letters and Documents,* Oxford 1995.
-----, *Christoph Willibald Gluck: a Guide to Research,* 2nd edition, London 2003.

HUTCHINGS, Arthur, *Gluck and Reform Opera,* essay accompanying Decca recording of Gluck's *Orfeo ed Euridice,* cond. Sir Georg Solti, SET.443/444, 1970.

LOWE, Alfonso, *La Serenissima: the Last Flowering of the Venetian Republic*, London 1974.

MITFORD, Nancy, *Frederick the Great*, London 1970.

MÜLLER VON ASOW, Hedwig and E. H., *The Collected Correspondence and Papers of Christoph Willibald Gluck*, tr. Stewart Thomson, London 1962.

NEWMAN, Ernest, *Gluck and the Opera: a Study in Musical History*, London 1895.

POPE, Alexander, *The Poems*, ed. John Butt, London 1963.

ROBINSON, Michael F., *Opera before Mozart*, London 1966.

ROSSELLI, John, *The Opera Industry in Italy from Cimarosa to Verdi: the Role of the Impresario*, Cambridge 1984.

SADIE, Stanley (ed.), *New Grove Dictionary of Music and Musicians*, 2nd edition, London 2001.

SCHMIDGALL, Gary, *Literature as Opera*, New York 1977.

SHERIDAN, Richard Brinsley, *The Critic*, ed. David Crane (New Mermaids), London 1989.

SMITH, Patrick J., *The Tenth Muse: a Historical Study of the Opera Libretto*, New York 1970.

STERN, Tiffany, *Rehearsal from Shakespeare to Sheridan*, Oxford 2000.

STRUNK, Oliver (selector and annotator), *Source Readings in Musical History: from Classical Antiquity to the Romantic Era*, London 1952.

SWANSTON, Hamish F. G., *In Defence of Opera*, London 1978.

Index of Names

A
Achillini, Claudio 28
Addison, Joseph 4, 65
Aeschylus 44
Amigoni, Jacopo xi
Angiolini, Gasparo iii, 46
Ariosto, Ludovico 15
Aristotle 4, 67
Arteaga, Esteban (Stefano) de iii, 66
Augustus Caesar xii, 44
Augustus II ('the Strong') of Saxony xi
Augustus III of Saxony xi
Avison, Charles 31

B
Baltimore, Lord x
Baron, Michel 35
Beattie, James iii
Bellini, Giovanni 49
Berlioz, Hector 69
Bernacchi, Antonio 37
Bibiena, Ferdinando Galli da 49, 62
Blainville, Charles de iii
Boethius 17
Bononcini, Giovanni 30
Botta, Bergonzo 10
Brizio, Serafino 62
Brown, John iii
Brown, Lancelot ('Capability') 53
Brühl, Count Heinrich von xii
Brumoy, Pierre 67
Burlington, Lord 53, 54
Burney, Charles 25
Buzzoleni, Giovanni 39

C
Caccini, Giulio 19
Caesar, Gaius Julius 7, 13
Calzabigi, Ranieri de' iii, xiv, xv, 28, 34
Cambert, Robert 45
Caracalla, Bassanius 33
Carissimi, Giacomo 28
Carter, Elizabeth x, xvii, xix
Cato, Marcus Porcius 13
Cesti, Antonio 28

Chambers, William 53
Chastellux, François Jean de xvi, xvii
Châtelet, Émilie du ix
Cherubini, Luigi 66
Cicero, Marcus Tullius 1
Coltellini, Marco xiv xvii
Cork, Earl of 67
Corneille, Pierre 35
Cortona (Domenico Cecchi) 39
Curti, Domenico ('Il Dentone')

D
Dacier, André 65
D'Alembert, Jean 27, 28, 39, 47
Dante Alighieri 36
Demosthenes 1
Diderot, Denis iii, xiii
Dryden, John 5, 65

E
Epictetus xvii
Escribano, Manuel xvii
Euripides 10, 67

F
Farinelli (Carlo Broschi) 6, 25
Ferrari, Defendente 47
Fielding, Henry iv
Fontenelle, Bernard de 27
Frangipane, Cornelio 10
Frederick the Great x, xi, xiii, 1, 6, 15, 64
Freschi, Orazio 4
Frescobaldi, Girolamo 30
Frugoni, Carlo Innocenzio xii

G
Galliari, Fabrizio iii
Galuppi, Baldassare 30
Garrick, David x, 35, 46
Genga, Girolamo 48
Giorgione (Giorgio da Castelfranco) 55
Gluck, Christoph Willibald iii, ix, xiii, xiv, xv, xix, 4, 9, 15, 20, 22, 24, 27, 28, 29, 30, 34, 39, 46, 52, 66, 67
Goldoni, Carlo xiv, xviii

Goldsmith, Oliver iv, xviii, xix
Graun, Carl Heinrich xi, 15, 66
Gravina, Gian Vincenzo 65
Gray, Thomas 6
Grimm, Melchior 39
Guadagni, Gaetano 6, 46

H
Handel, George Frideric vii, viii, 15, 30
Hasse, Johann Adolf 30
Hemmerde, Johann Friedrich xvii
Henry III of France 10
Hill, Aaron 35
Homer xii
Horace (Quintus Horatius Flaccus) 4, 40, 41
Hume, David x

J
Johnson, Samuel vii, 67
Jommelli, Niccolò viii, 30, 45

K
Kent, William 53
Kneller, Godfrey 5

L
La Harpe, Jean François de 66
Lecouvreur, Adrienne 35
Legrenzi, Giovanni 33
Le Gros, Joseph, 39
Lennox, Charlotte 67
Le Nôtre, André 53
Leopold, Archduke of Tuscany xv
Levasseur, Rosalie 39
Licinius 50, 51
Longinus 27
Lorrain, Claude 54
Louis XIV 11
Lully, Jean-Baptiste xii, 11, 14, 15, 20

M
Mantegna, Andrea 49
Marcello, Benedetto viii, 30, 31, 36, 65
Marchesi, Luigi 6
Marini, Giambattista 28, 36, 37
Maupertuis, Pierre ix
Mazarin, Cardinal Jules de 11

Ménage, Gilles 56
Merulo, Claudio 10
Metastasio (Pietro Trapassi) viii, xviii, 15, 20, 28, 52, 65
Molière, Jean-Baptiste 35, 56
Montagu, Lady Mary Wortley x
Monteverdi, Claudio 28
Mouret, Jean-Joseph 45
Mozart, Wolfgang Amadeus iii, vii, xiv, 37
Muratori, Ludovico Antonio xviii, 65
Musi, Maria Maddalena 12

N
Newton, Isaac ix, x, xiii, xvii
Nicolini (Niccolò Grimaldi) 36
Norden, Frederick Ludvig 51
Noverre, Jean-Georges 46

O
Orlandini, Giovanni Maria 45
Ovid (Publius Ovidius Naso) xiii, 40

P
Palestrina, Giovanni Pierluigi da 30
Palladio, Andrea 54, 64
Pasquali, Giambattista xvii
Pausanias 17
Pergolesi, Giovanni Battista 29, 39
Peri, Jacopo 10, 21
Pericles 7
Pericoli, Niccolò ('Il Tribulo') 47
Perruzzi, Baldassare 48
Perugini (Pietro Vannucci) 49
Petrarch (Francesco Petrarca) 27, 28
Piazzetta, Giovanni Battista xi
Piccinni, Niccolò 29
Pistocchi, Francesco 36, 37
Pitt, William the Elder xv, 1
Pittoni, Giovanni Battista xi
Planelli, Antonio iii
Poliziano, Angelo 10
Pope, Alexander x, 54
Pozzo, Andrea 51
Pozzo, Girolamo del 64
Pylades 44, 45

Q
Quinault, Philippe 20

R
Rameau, Jean-Philippe xii, xviii, 45, 66
Raphael (Raffaello Sanzio) 48
Rembrandt (Harmenzsoon) van Rijn 55
Ricci, Marchetto 54
Rinuccini, Ottavio 9
Rodio, Rocco 30
Romano, Giulio 47
Roscius Gallus, Quintus 35
Roullet, François Louis du iii, xiii, 39

S
St. Évremond, Charles de 5
Salvini, Anton Maria 33
Sangallo, Antonio da 48
Sanmicheli, Michele 64
Sansovino (Andrea Contucci) 64
Scarlatti, Alessandro 23, 30
Scarlatti, Domenico 23
Segneri, Paolo 54
Septimius Severus 33, 63
Serlio, Sebastiano 48, 49
Sheridan, Richard Brinsley vii
Siface (Francesco Grossi) 39
Sighizzi, Andrea 62
Smollett, Tobias iv
Sophocles 10
Suard, Jean-Baptiste 66
Sweerts, Baron von xv

T
Tartini, Giuseppe 27
Tasso, Torquato 15

Temanza, Tommaso 64
Tesi-Tramontini, Vittoria 35
Tiepolo, Giambattista xi, xii
Tillot, Guillaume du xii
Timotheus of Miletus 17
Titian (Tiziano Veccello) 54, 55
Torelli, Giacomo 64
Tosi, Pierfrancesco 39
Traetta, Tommaso iii, viii, xii, xiii, xiv

U
Udine, Giovanni da 52

V
Veronese, Paolo 49, 50, 54
Vignola, Giacomo da 49
Vinci, Leonardo 20, 23, 30
Virgil (Publius Vergilius Maro) 23, 67, 69
Vitruvius 50, 58, 59
Voltaire (François-Marie Arouet) ix, x, 66

W
Wagner, Richard xiii, 66
Wallis, John 40
Webb, Daniel 19, 27
Winckelmann, Johann Joachim iv, 9

X
Xenophon 5

Z
Zarlino, Gioseffo 10
Zeno, Apostolo viii, xviii, 66